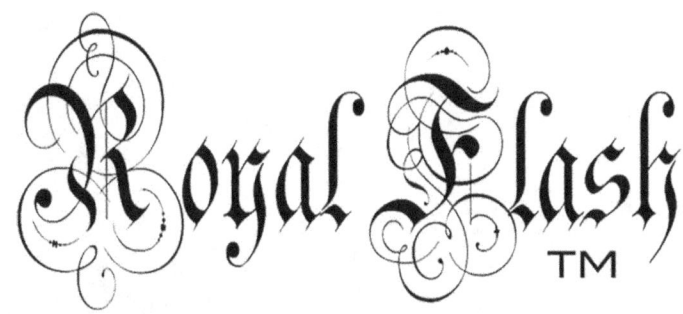

Presents

"Rock n Roll"
Tattoo Coloring Book

All Artwork by

Cort Bengtson

Published by

Cort's Royal Ink Tattoo Company

Book Design and Layout by

Cort Bengtson

Copyright 2017

All images are on file with

The Library of Congress

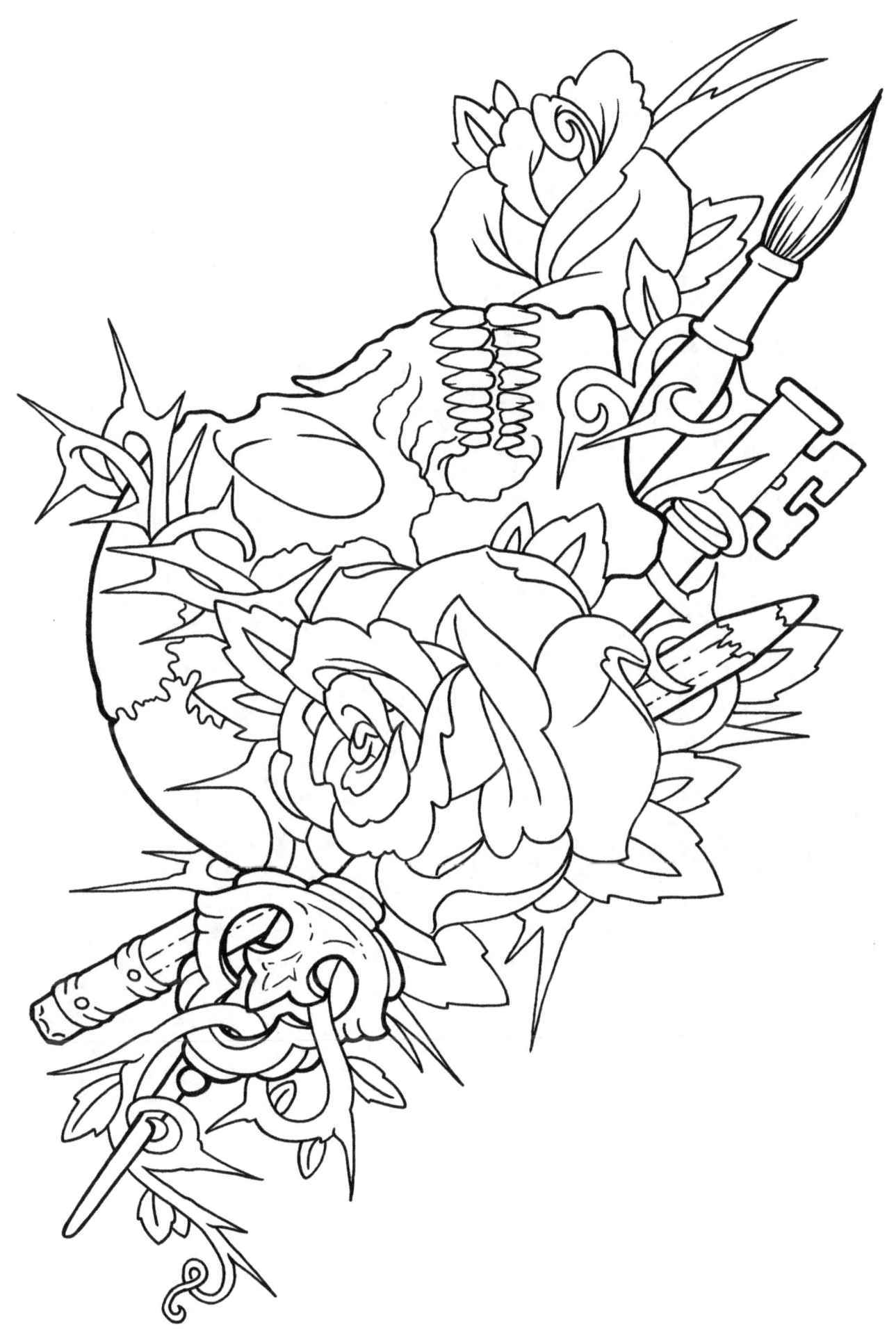

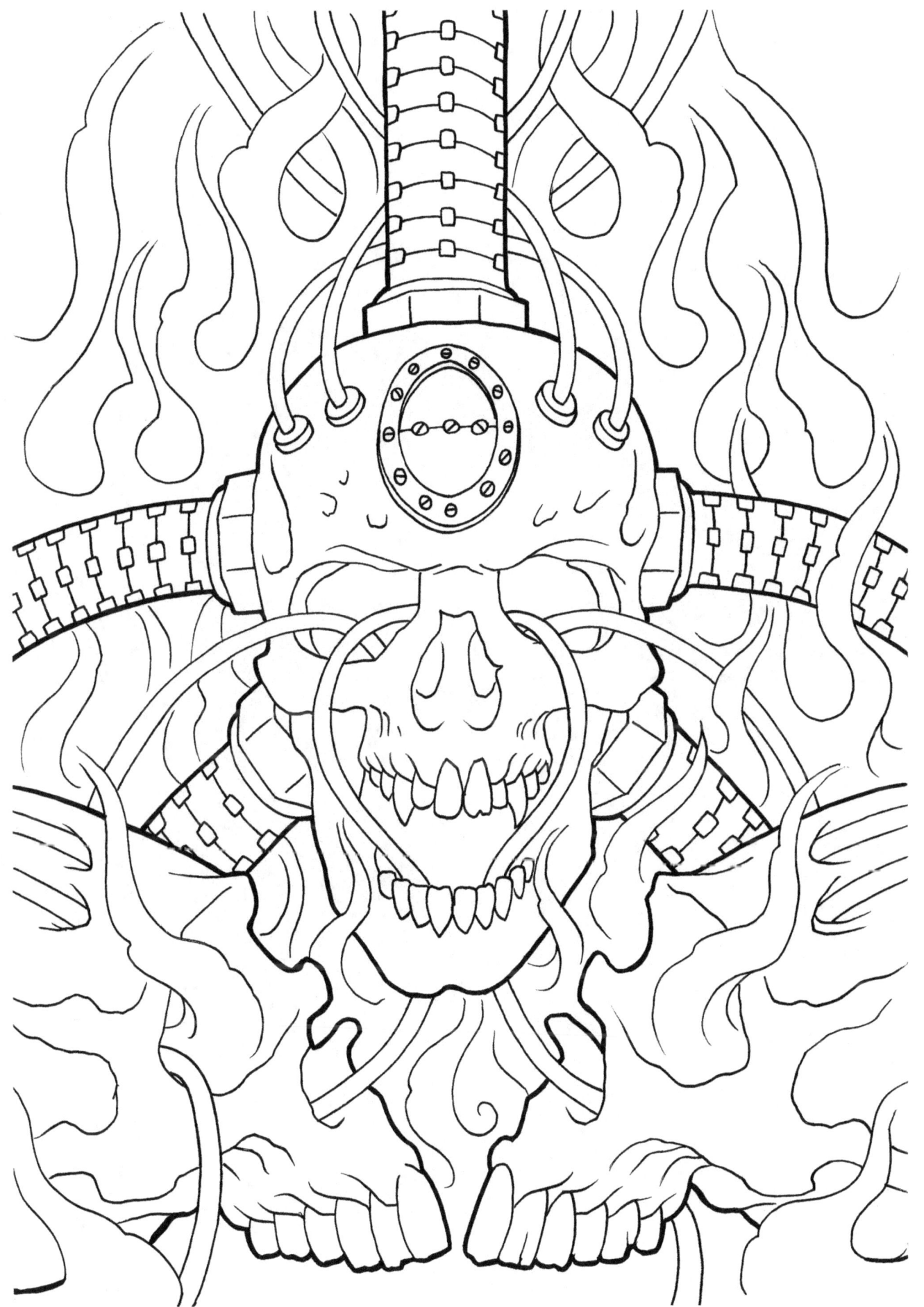

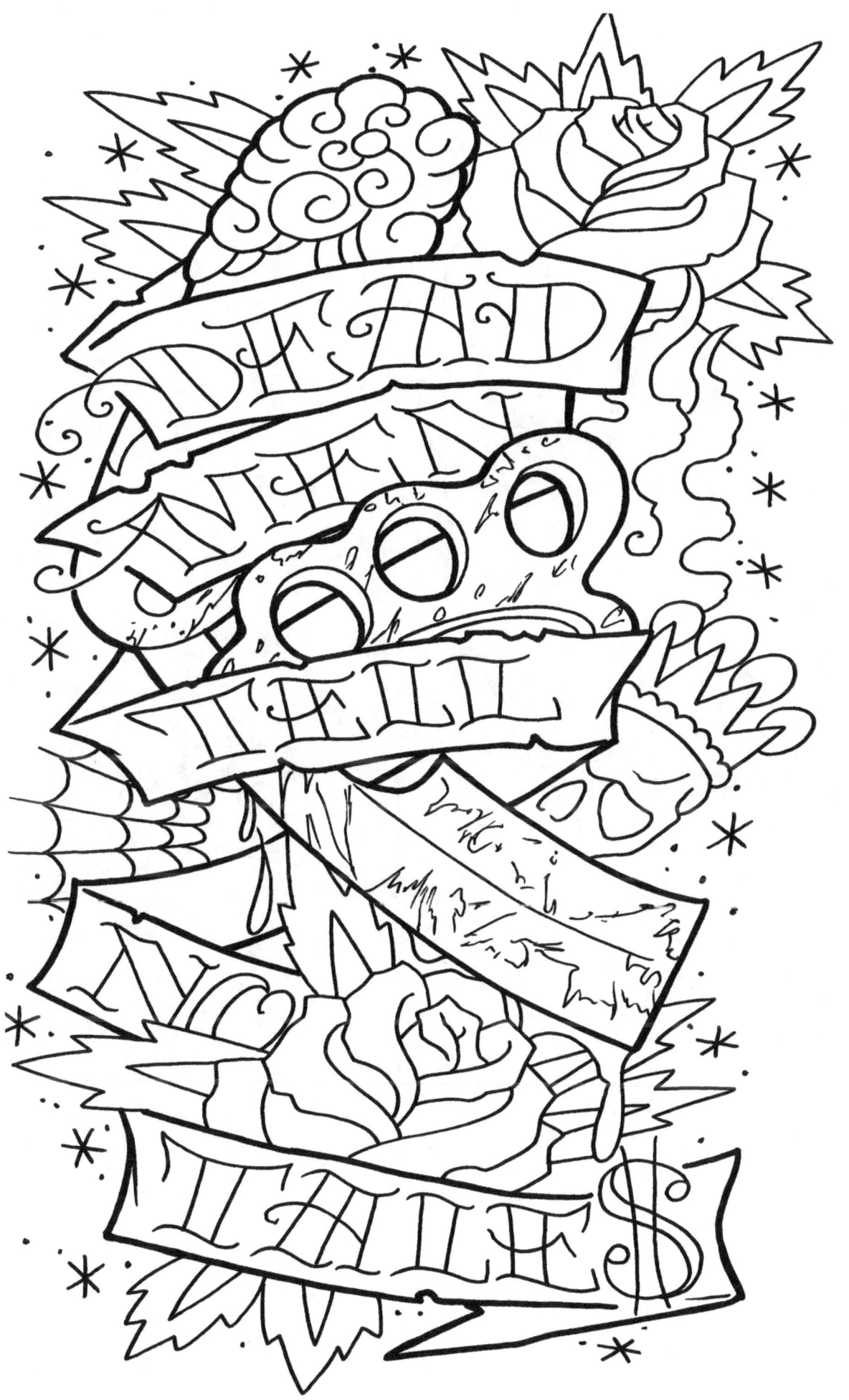

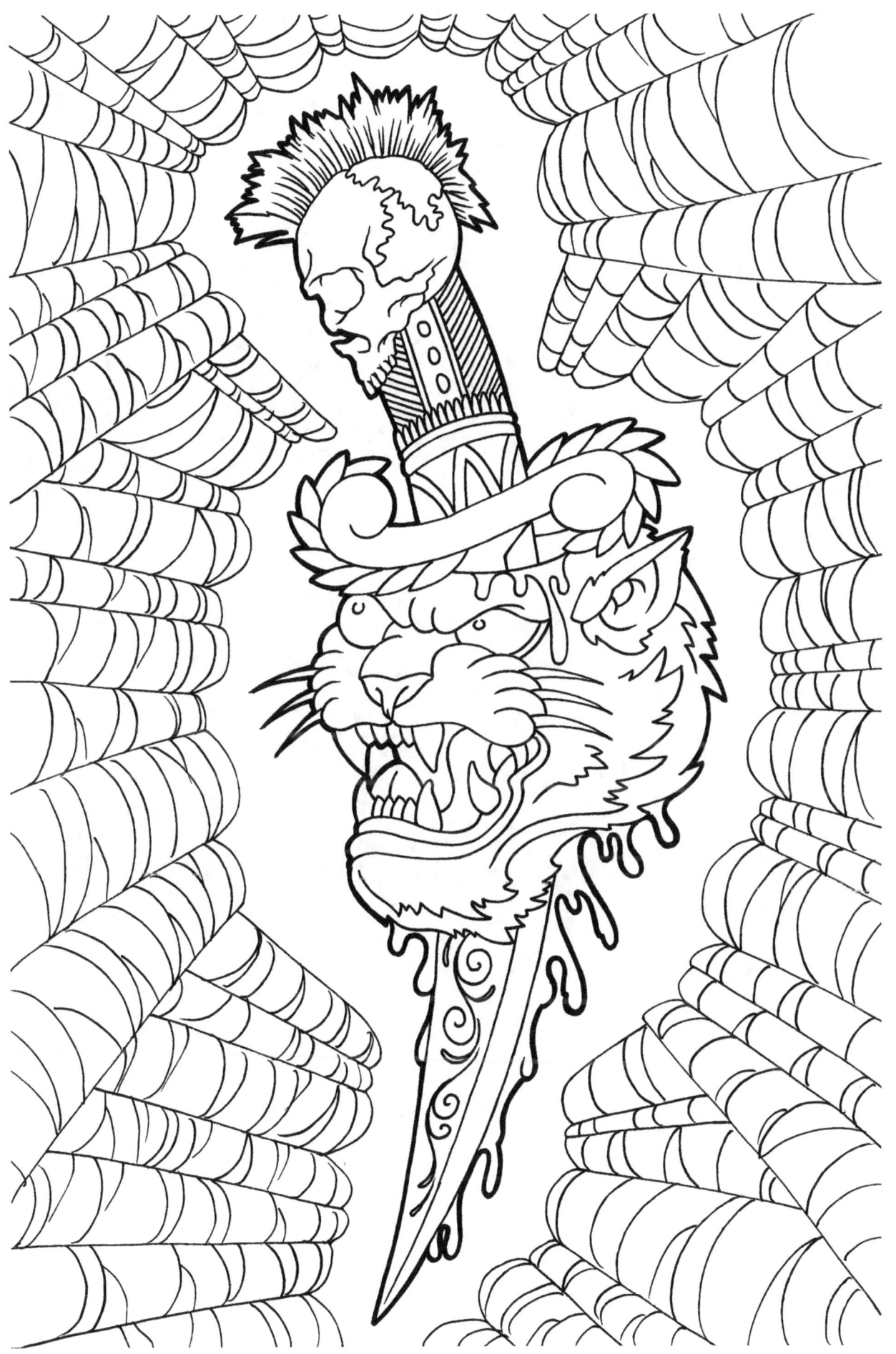

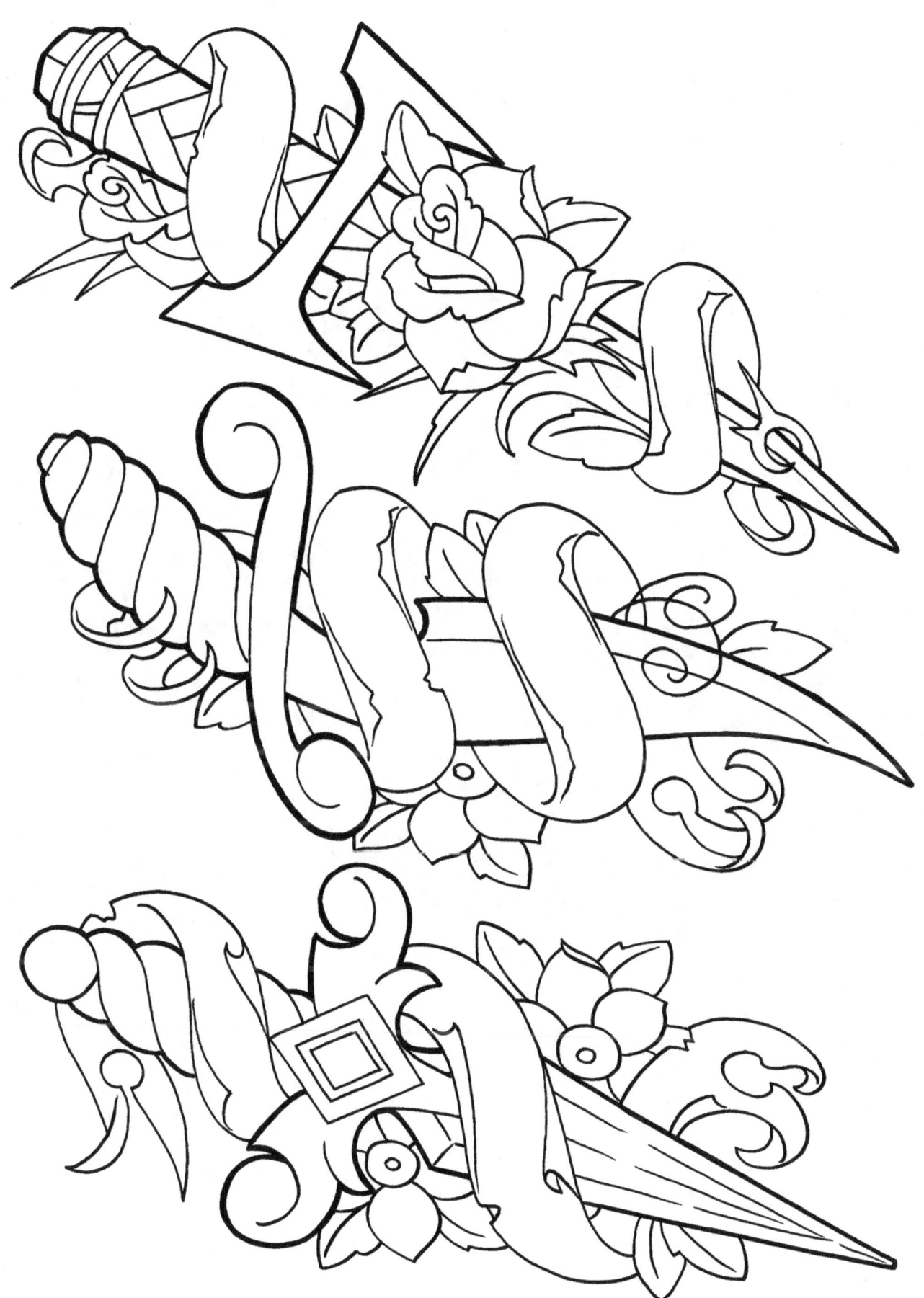

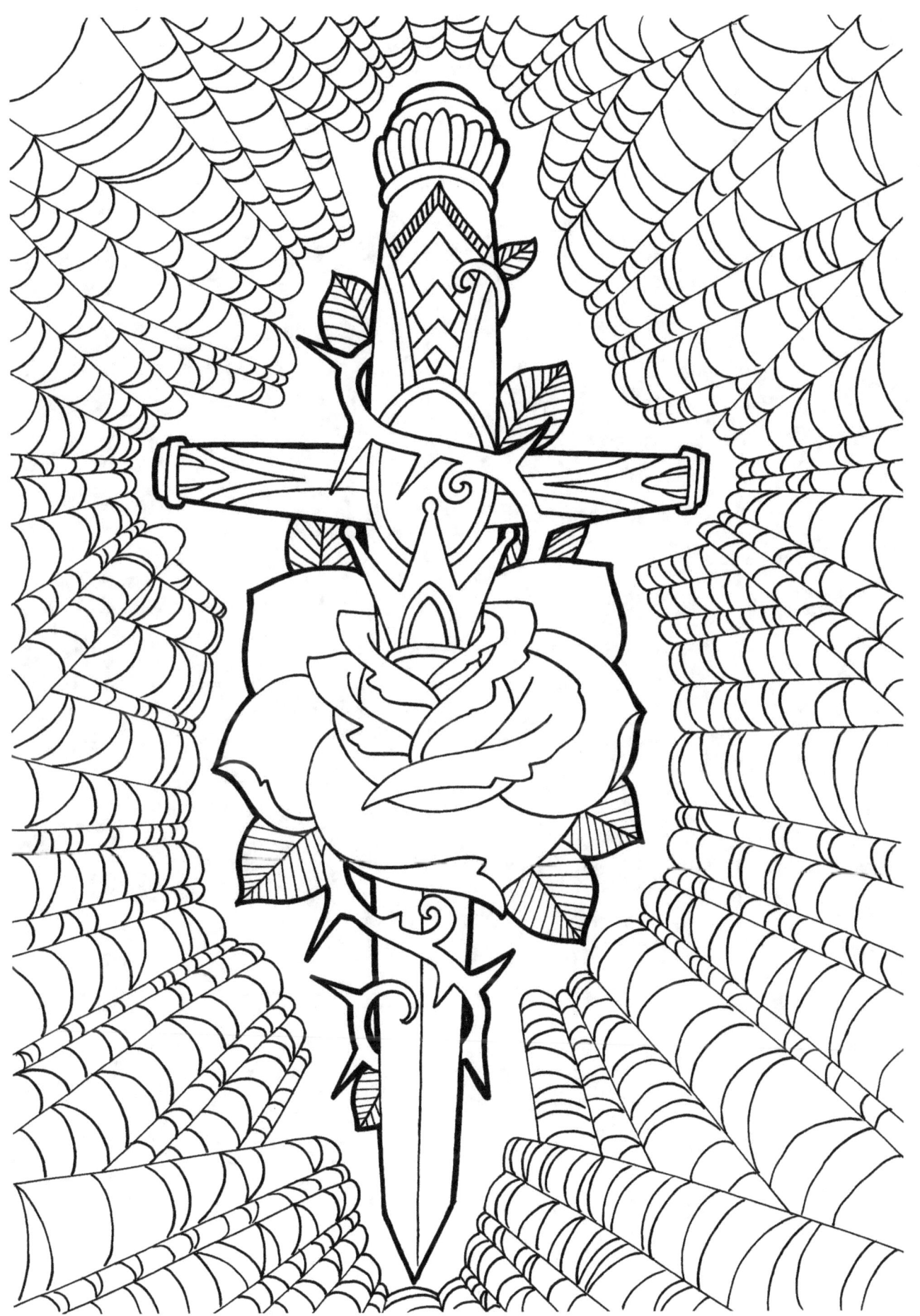

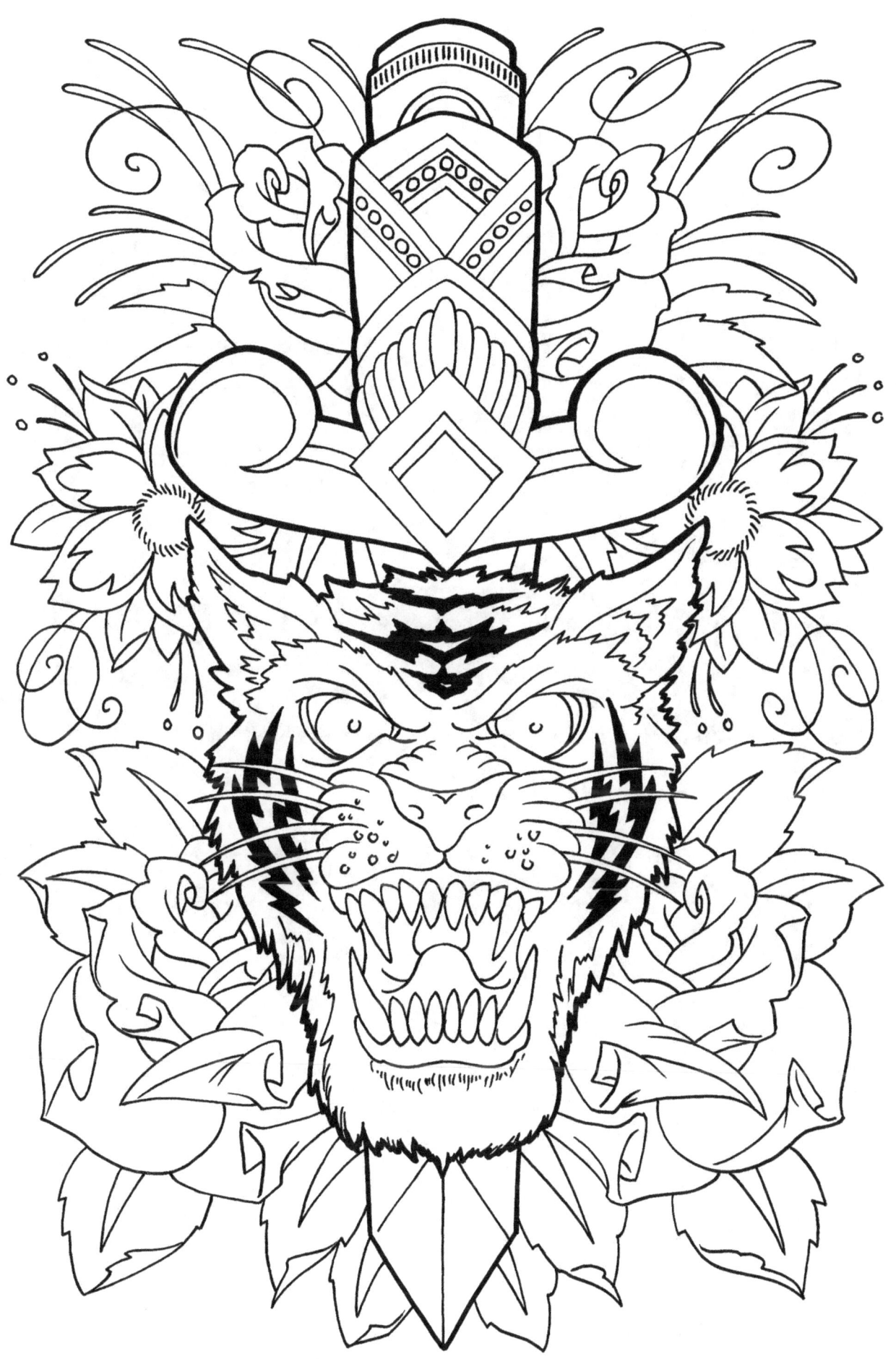

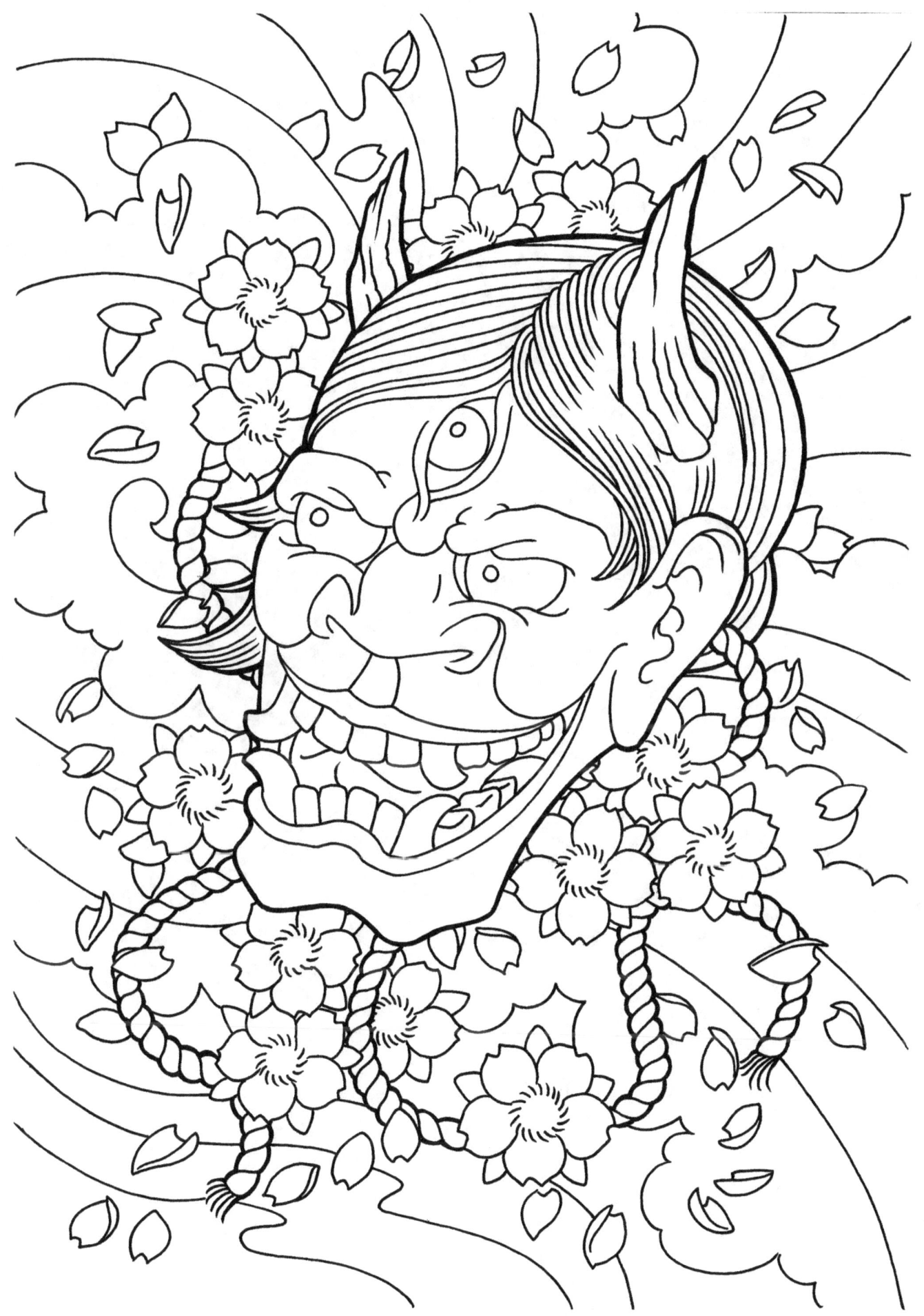

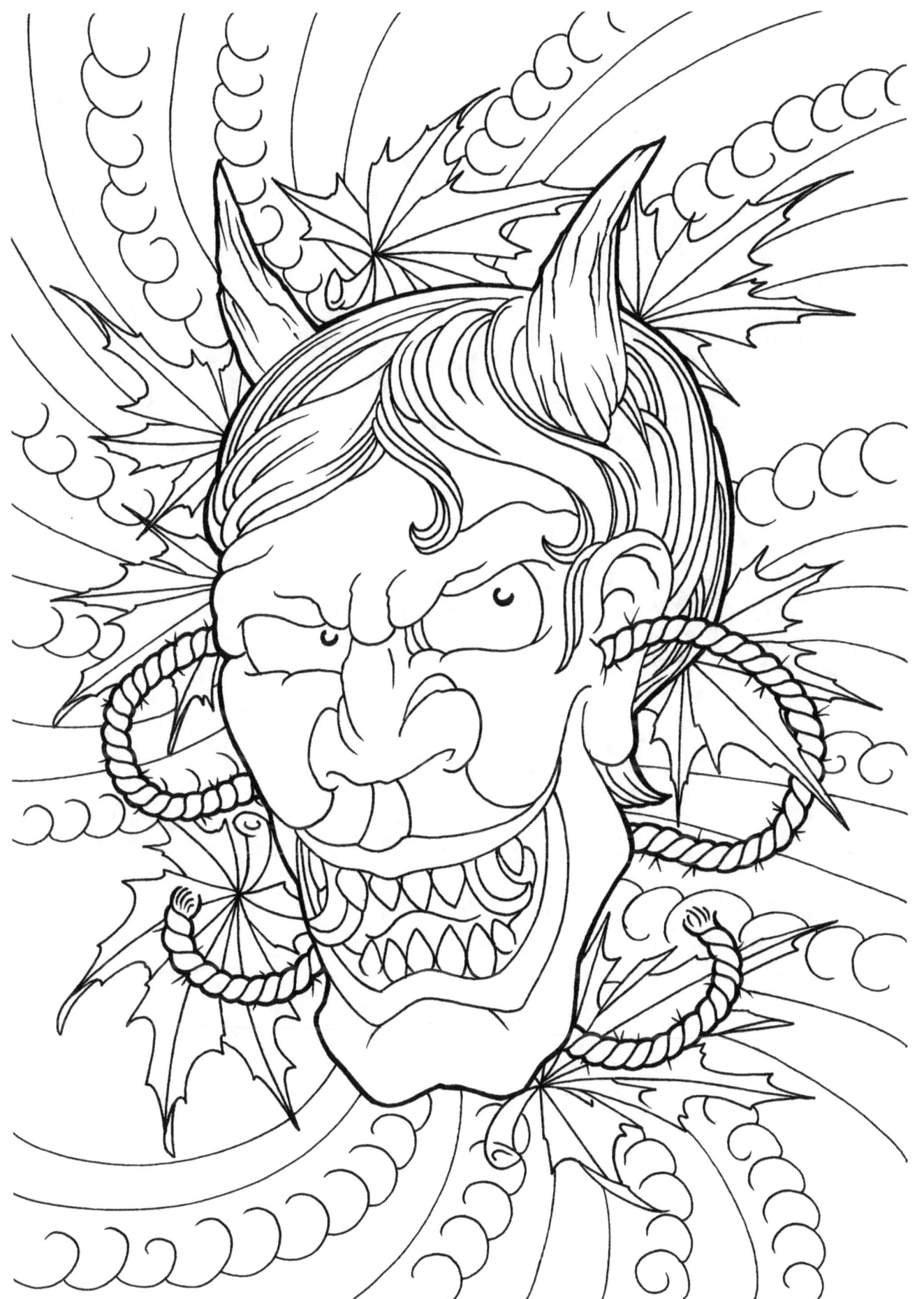

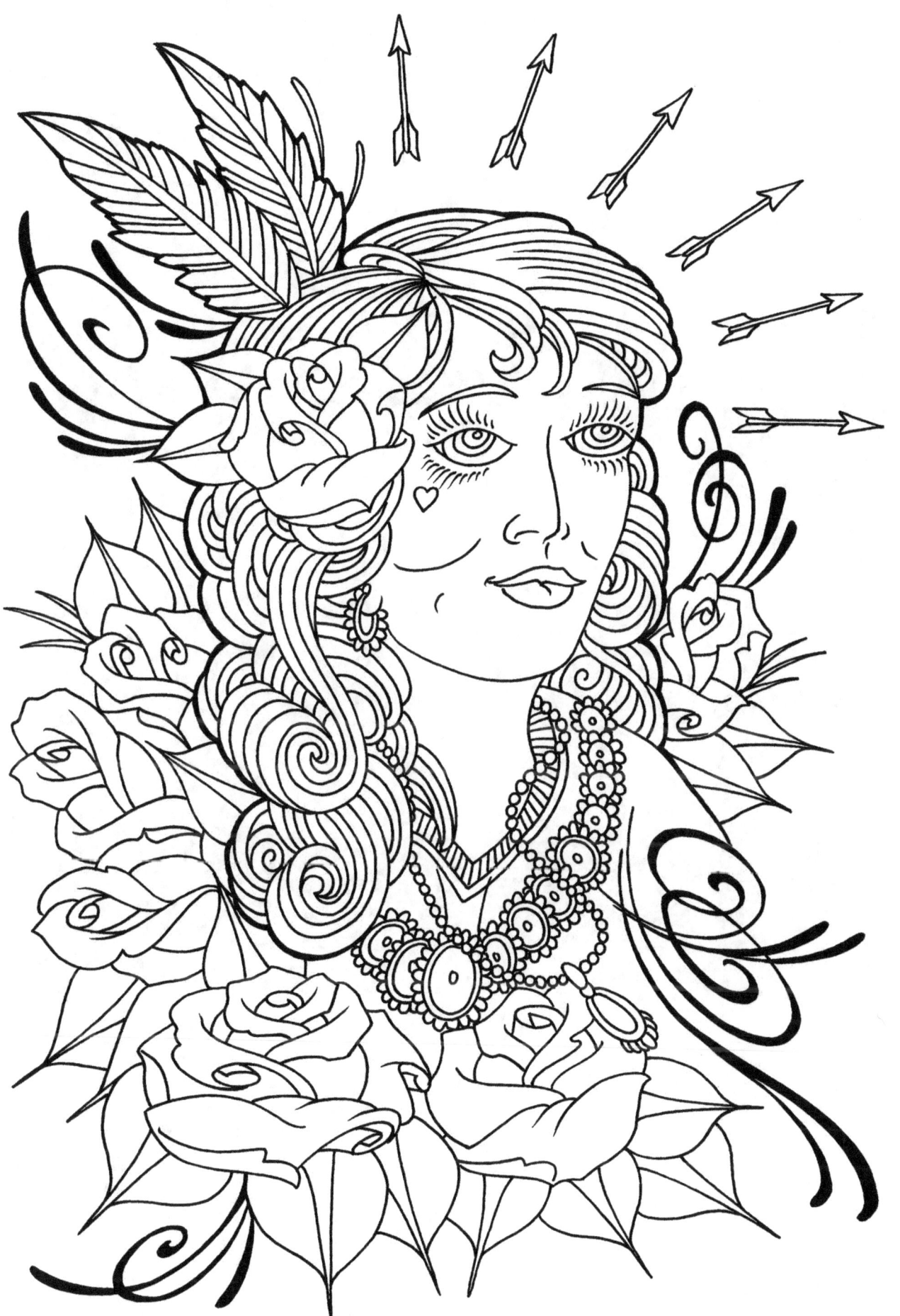

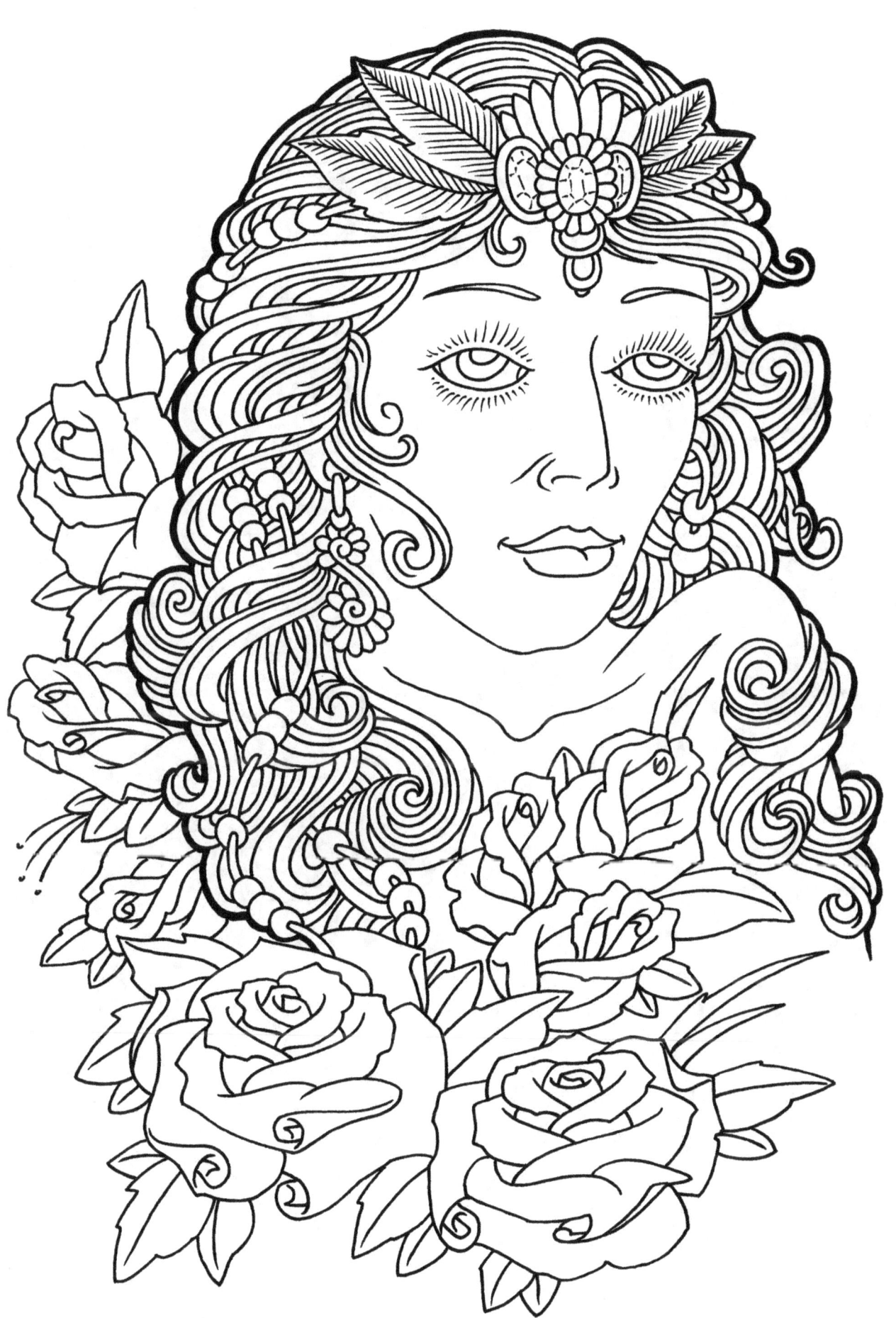

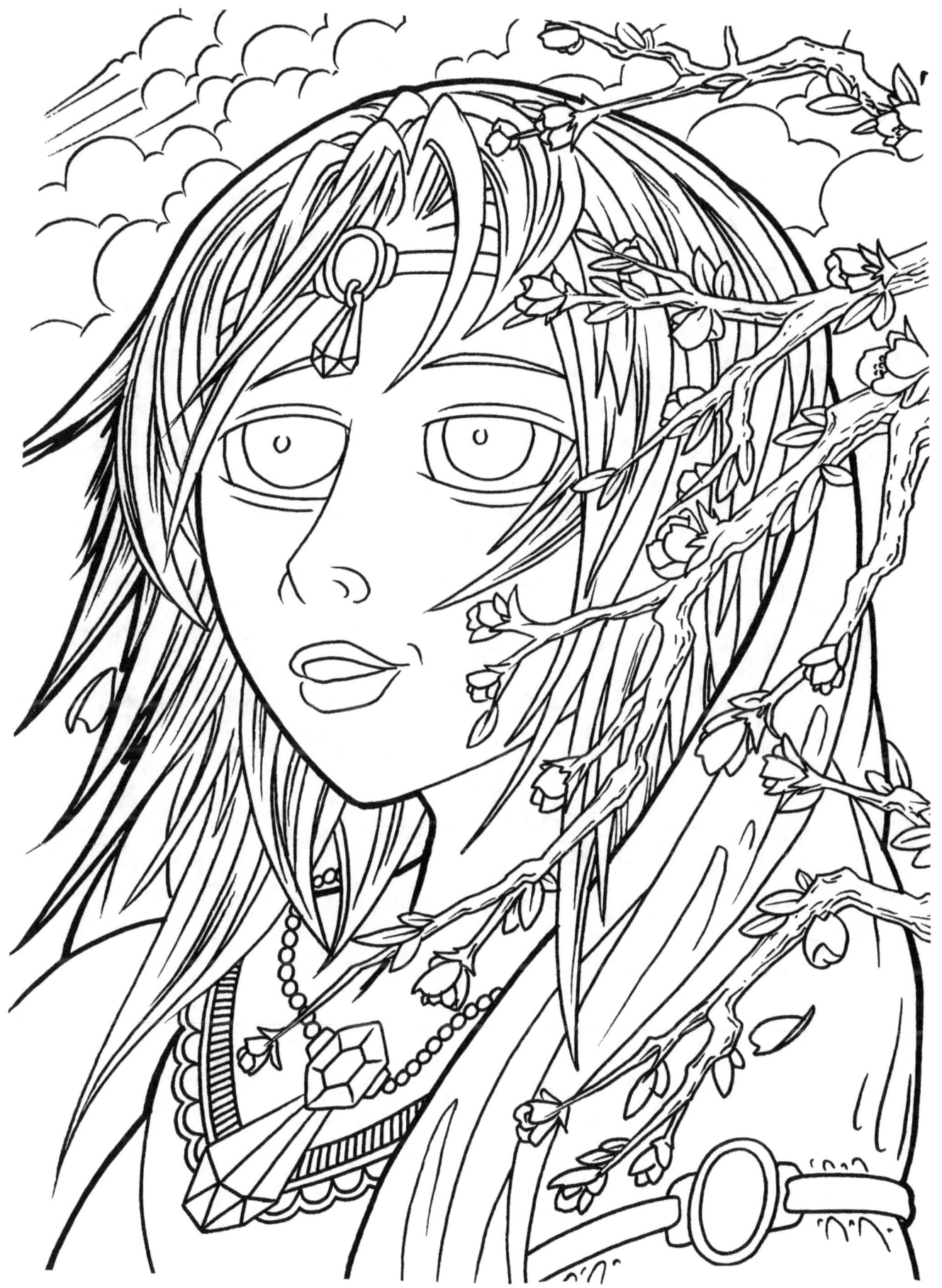

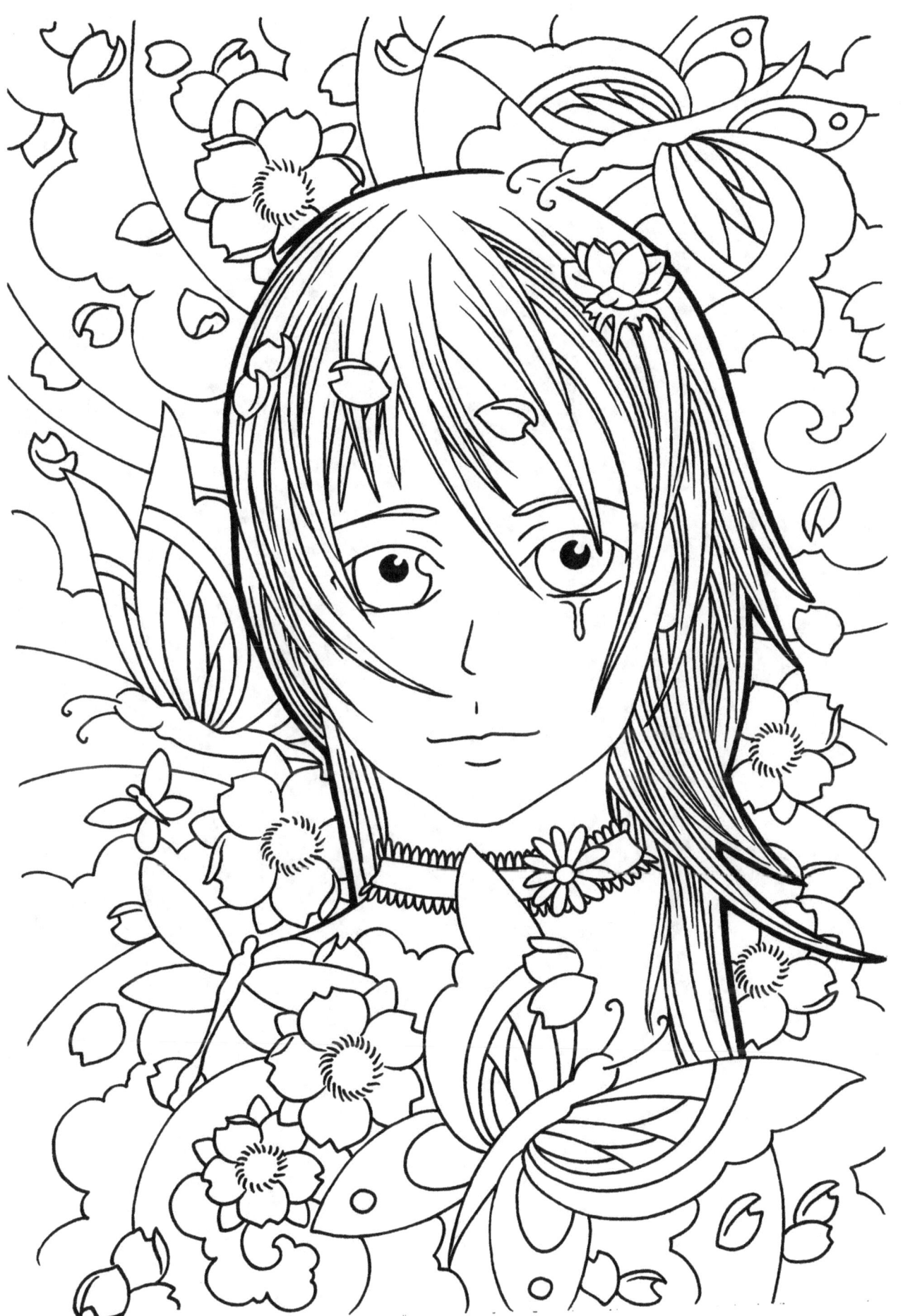

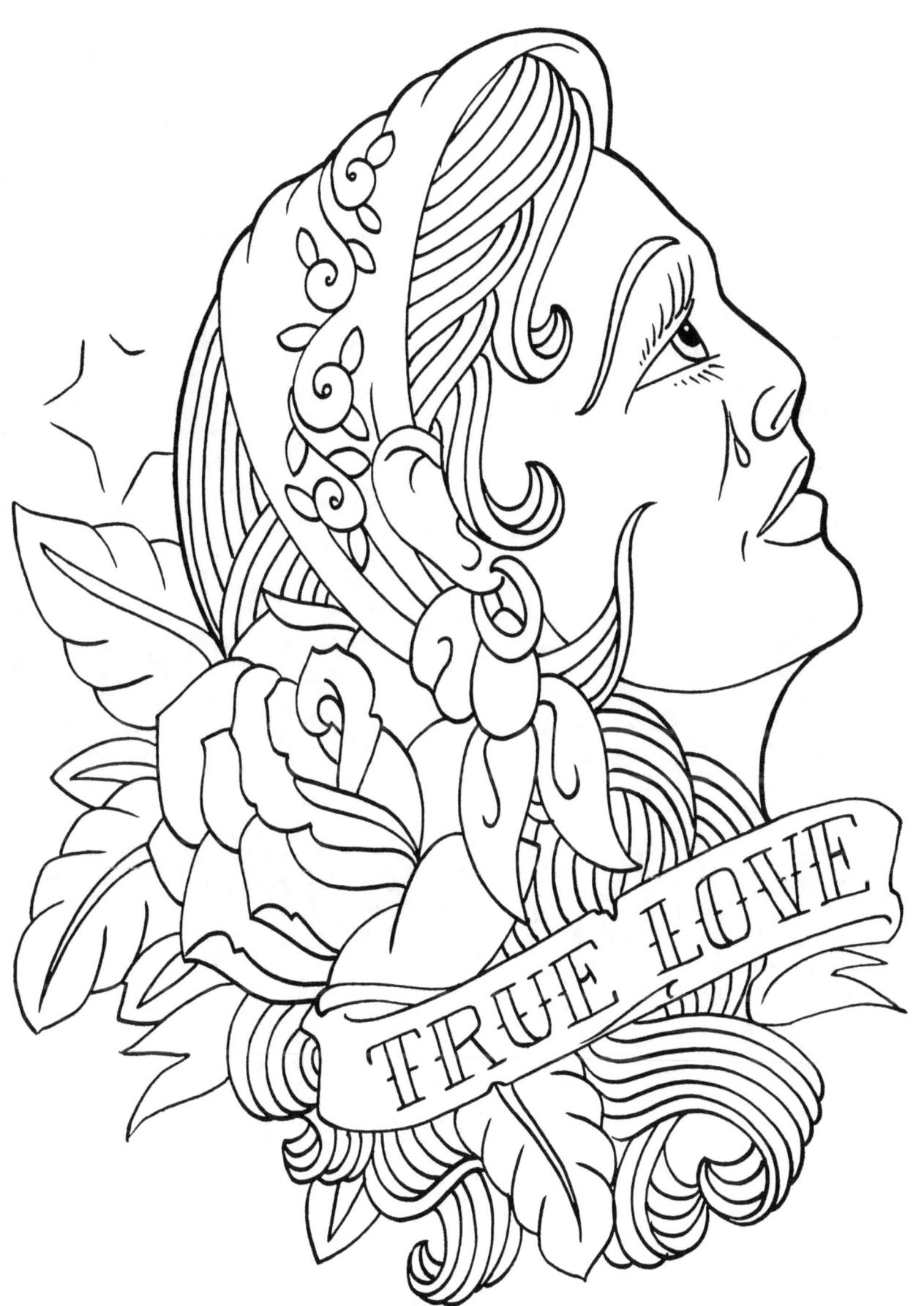

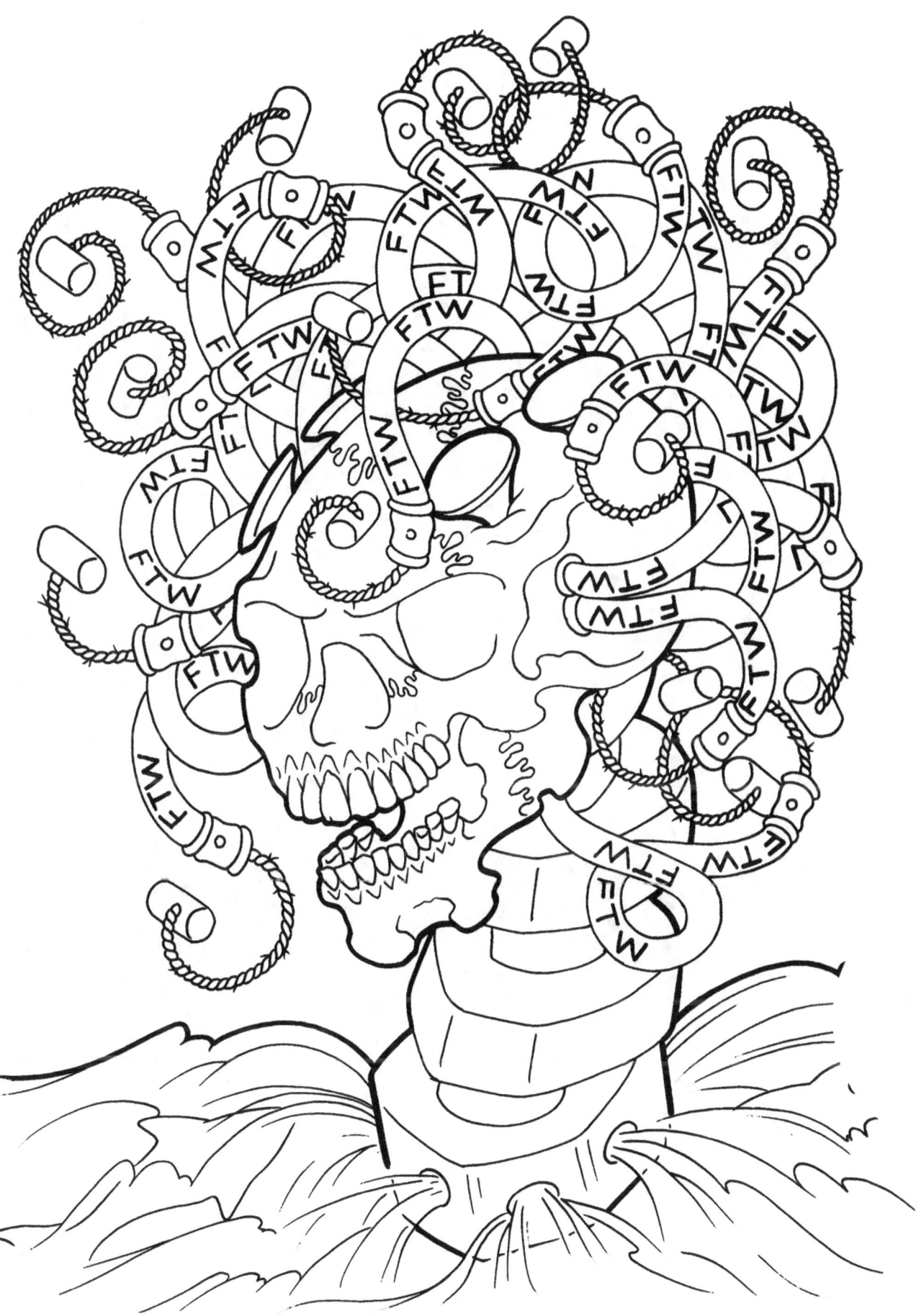

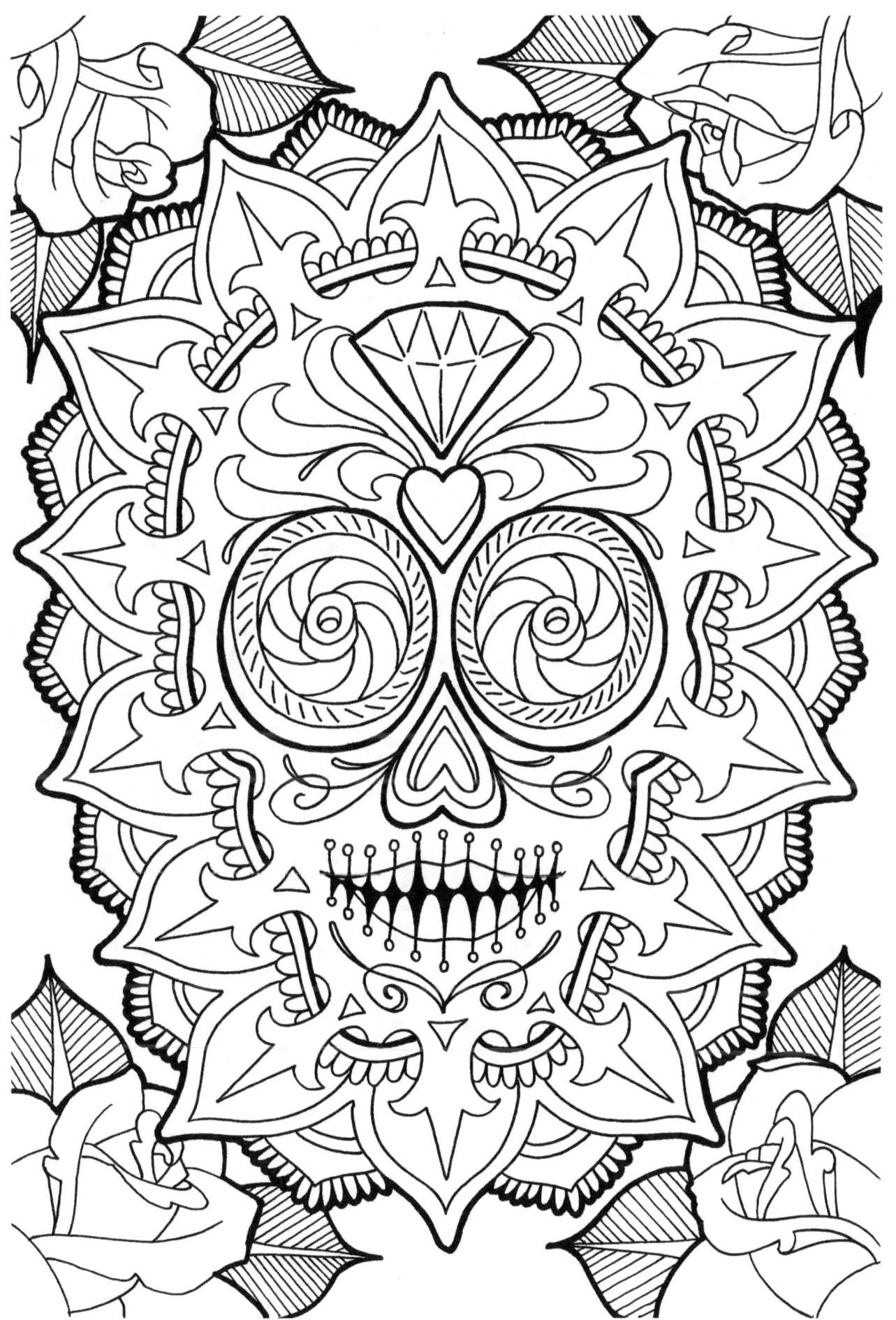

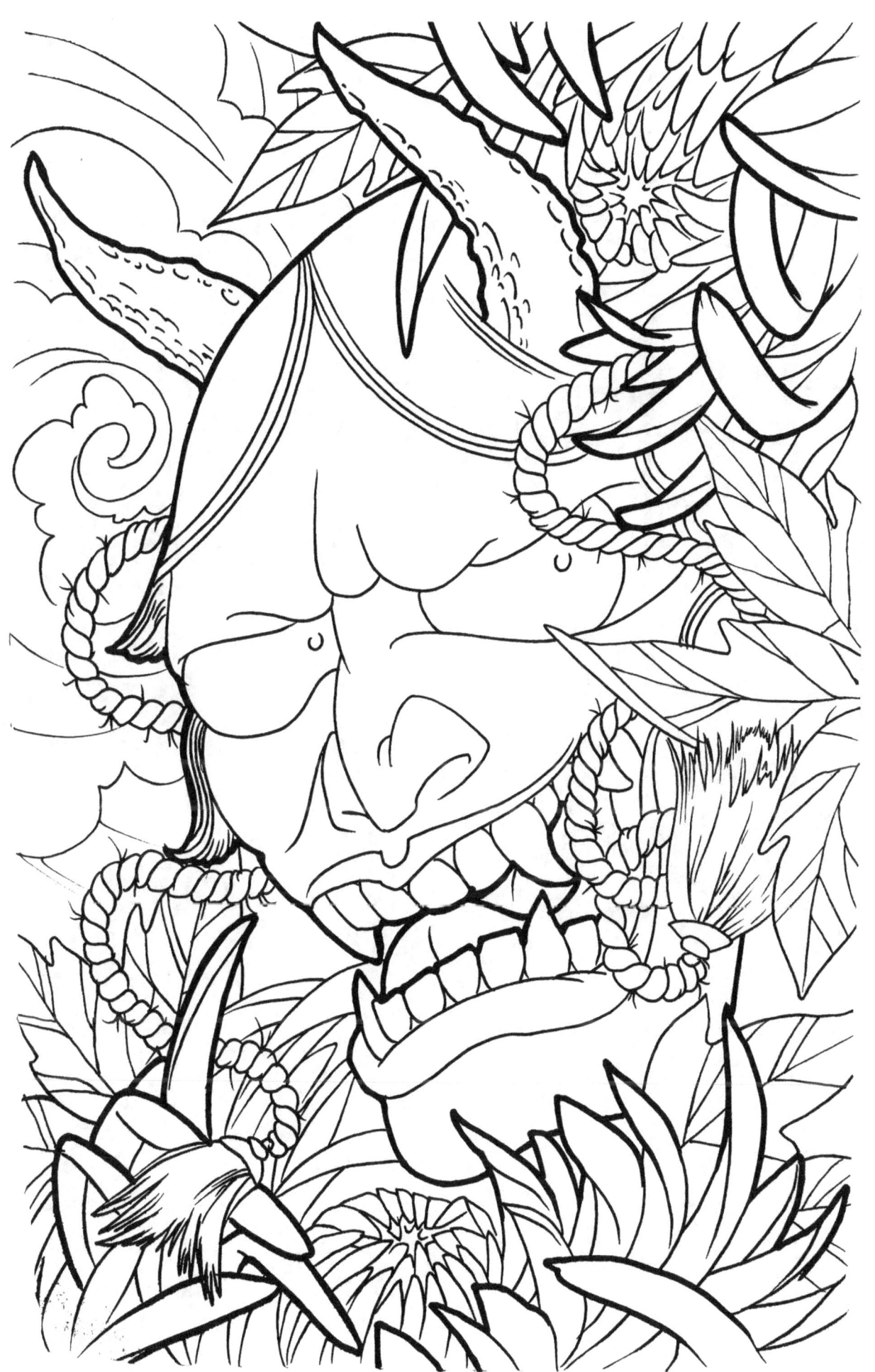

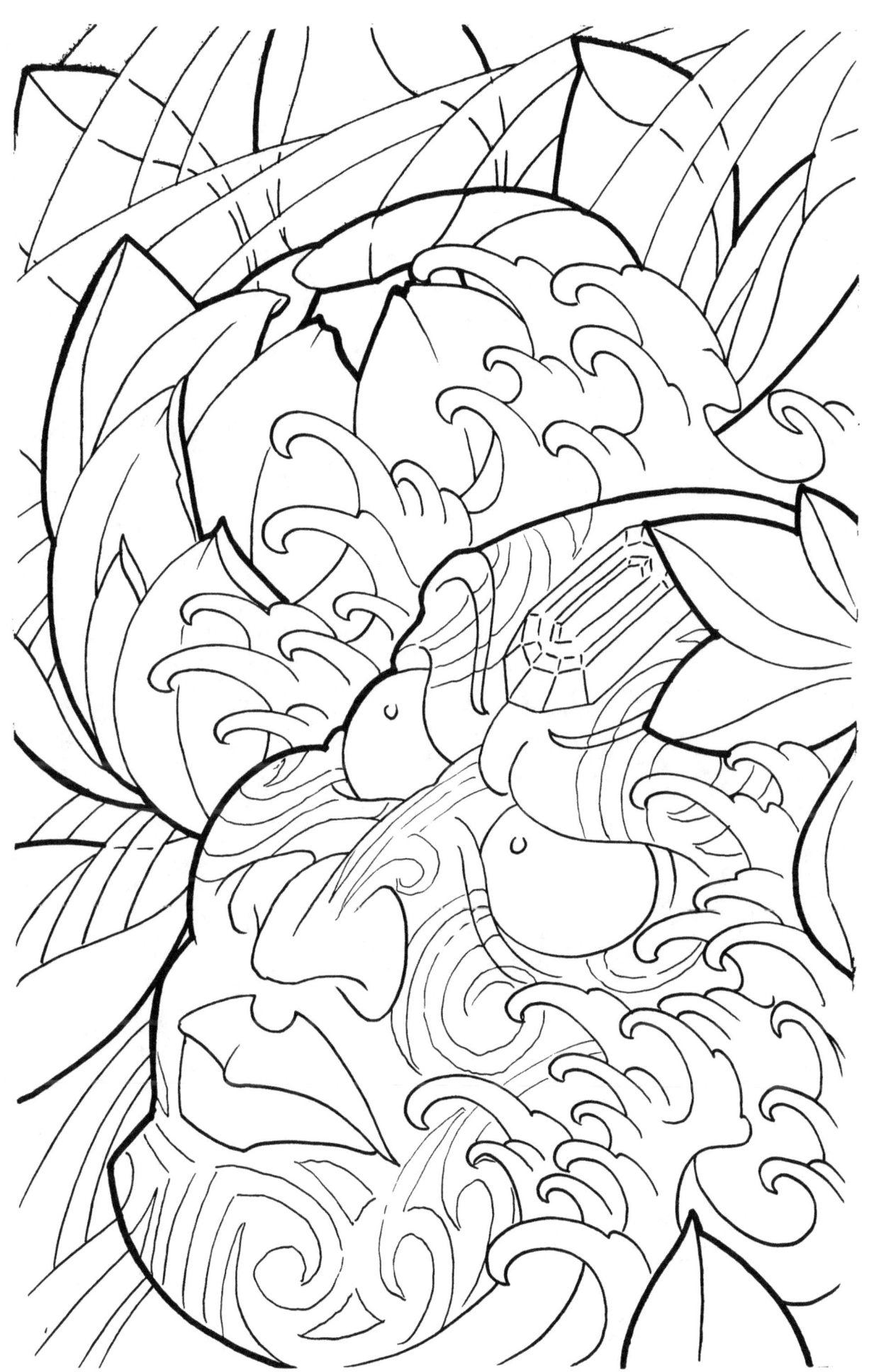

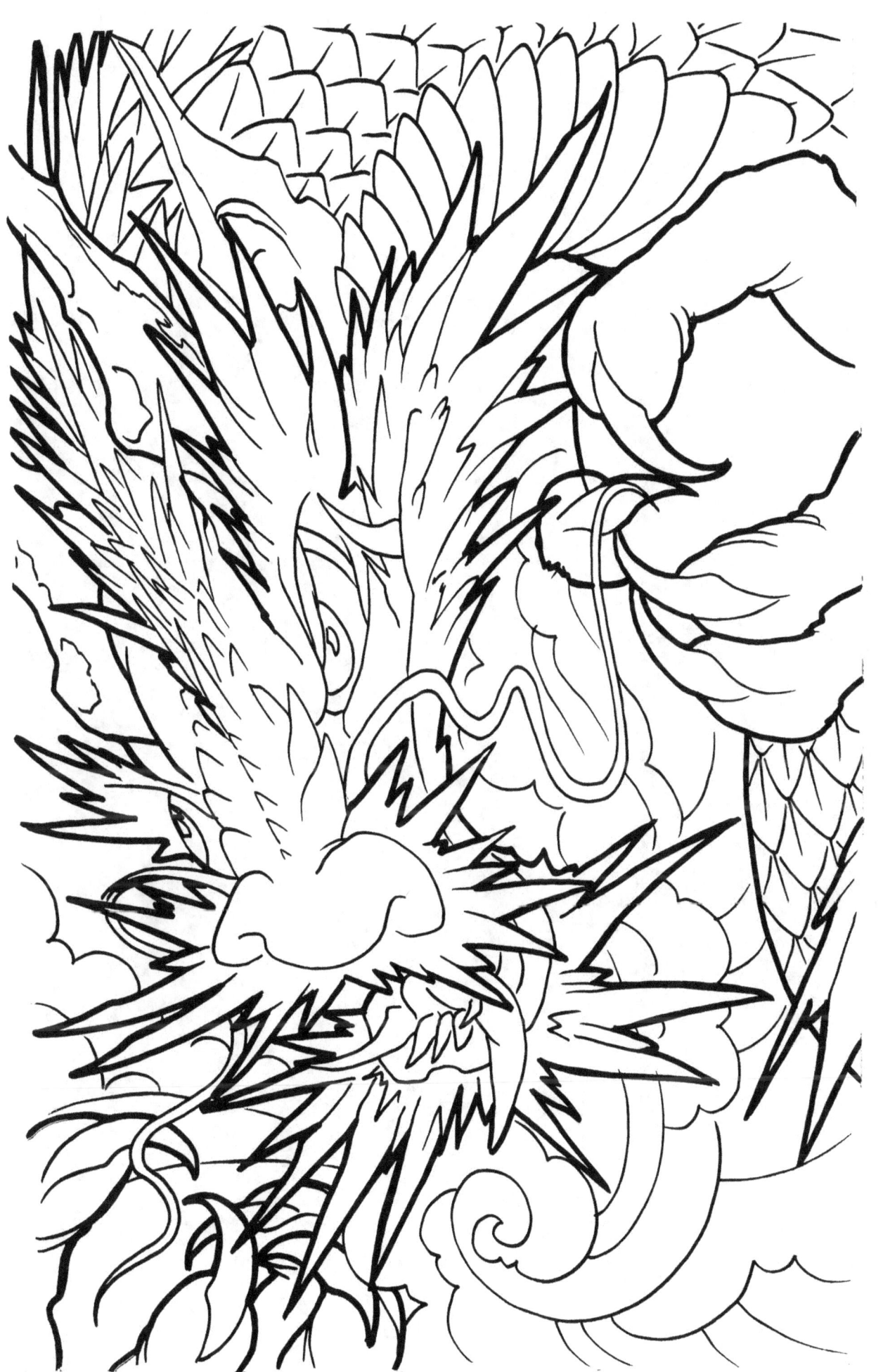

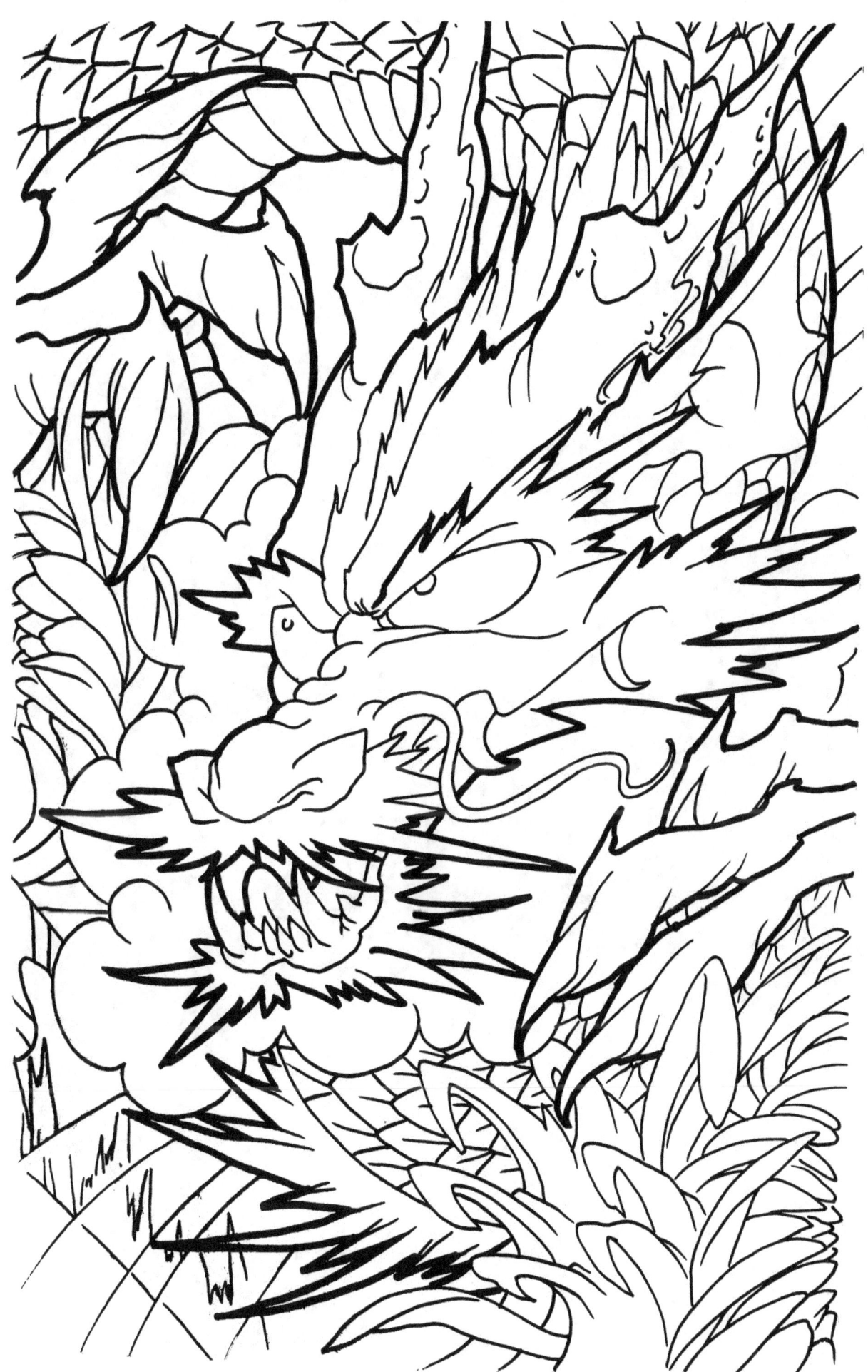

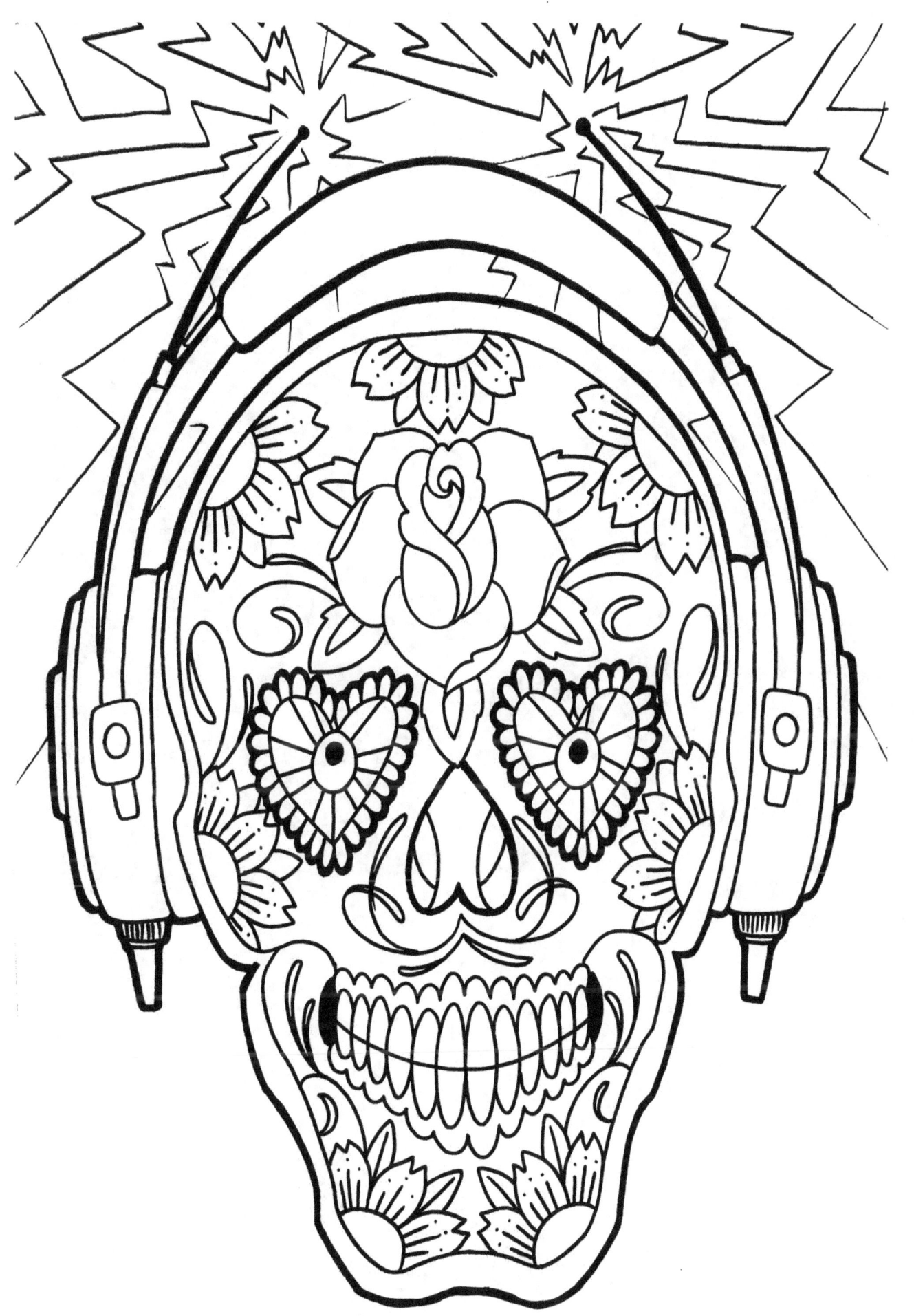

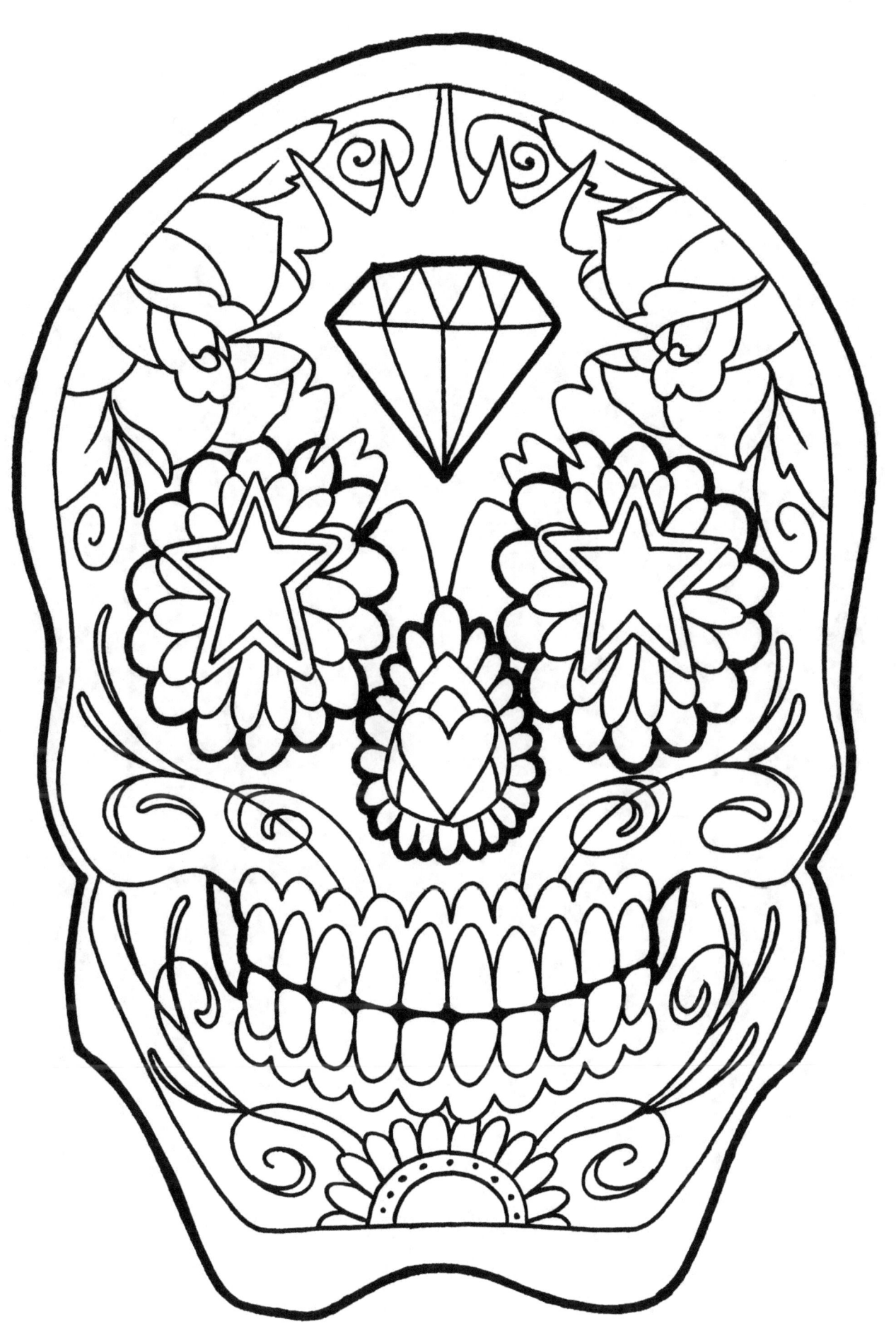

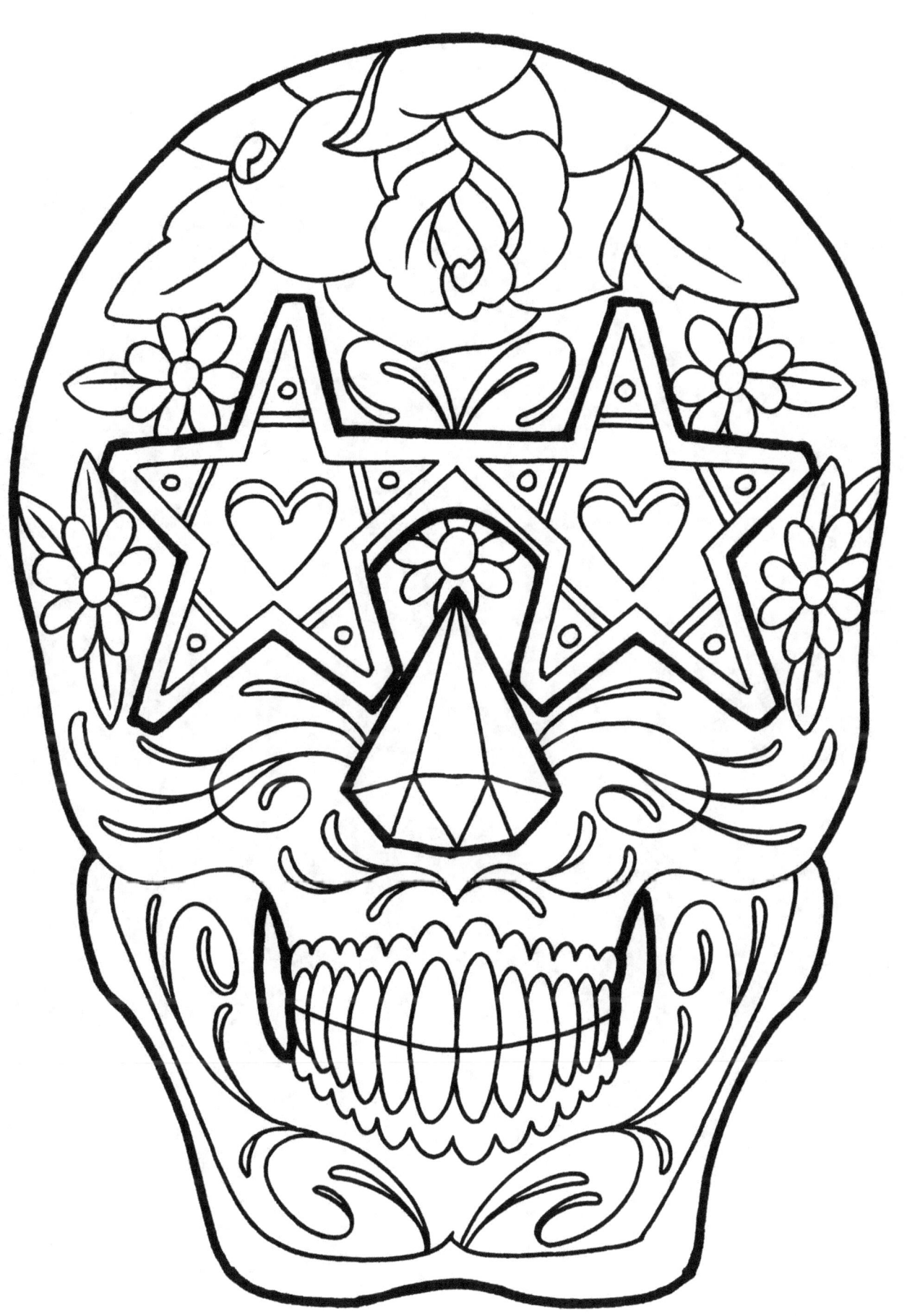

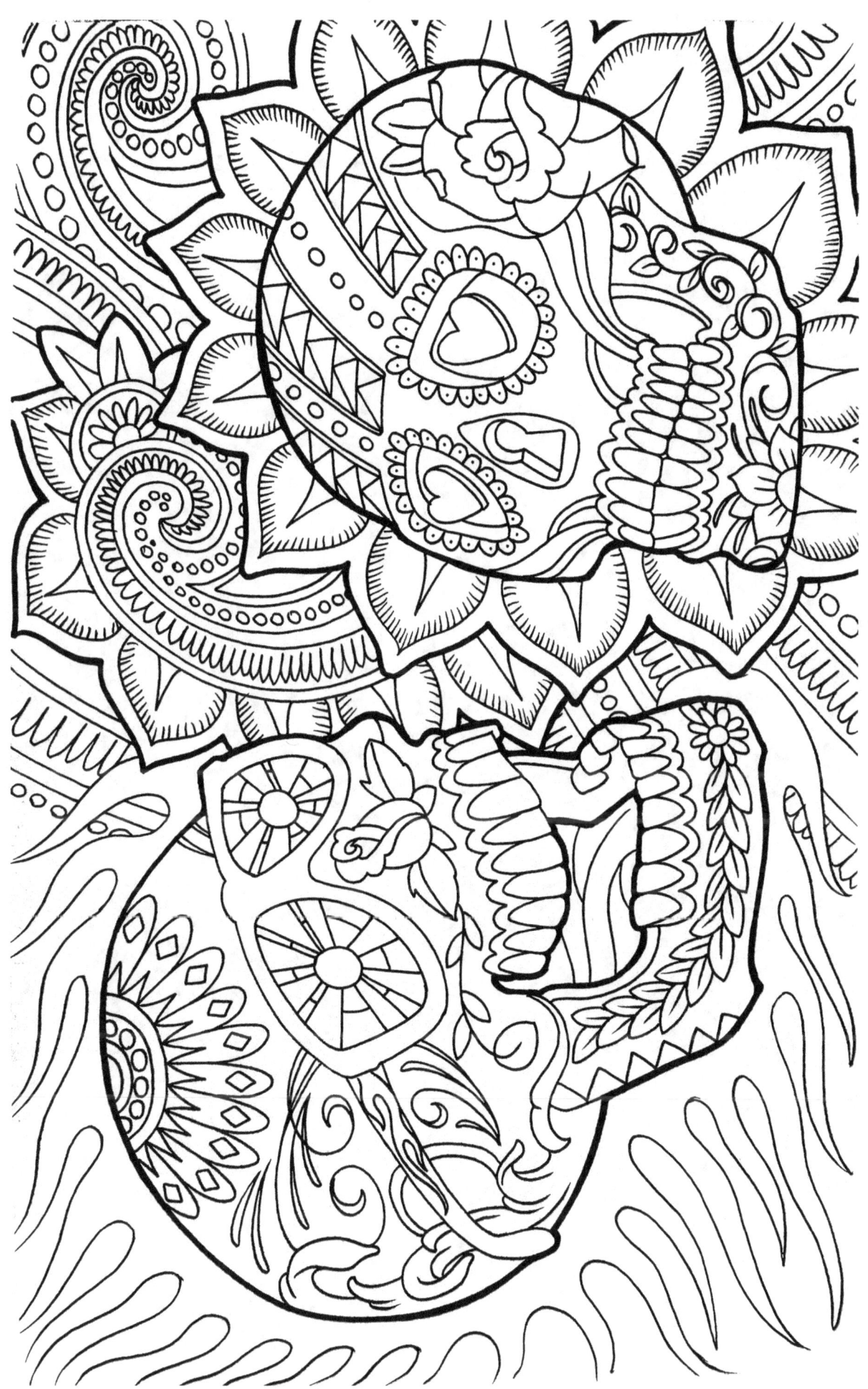

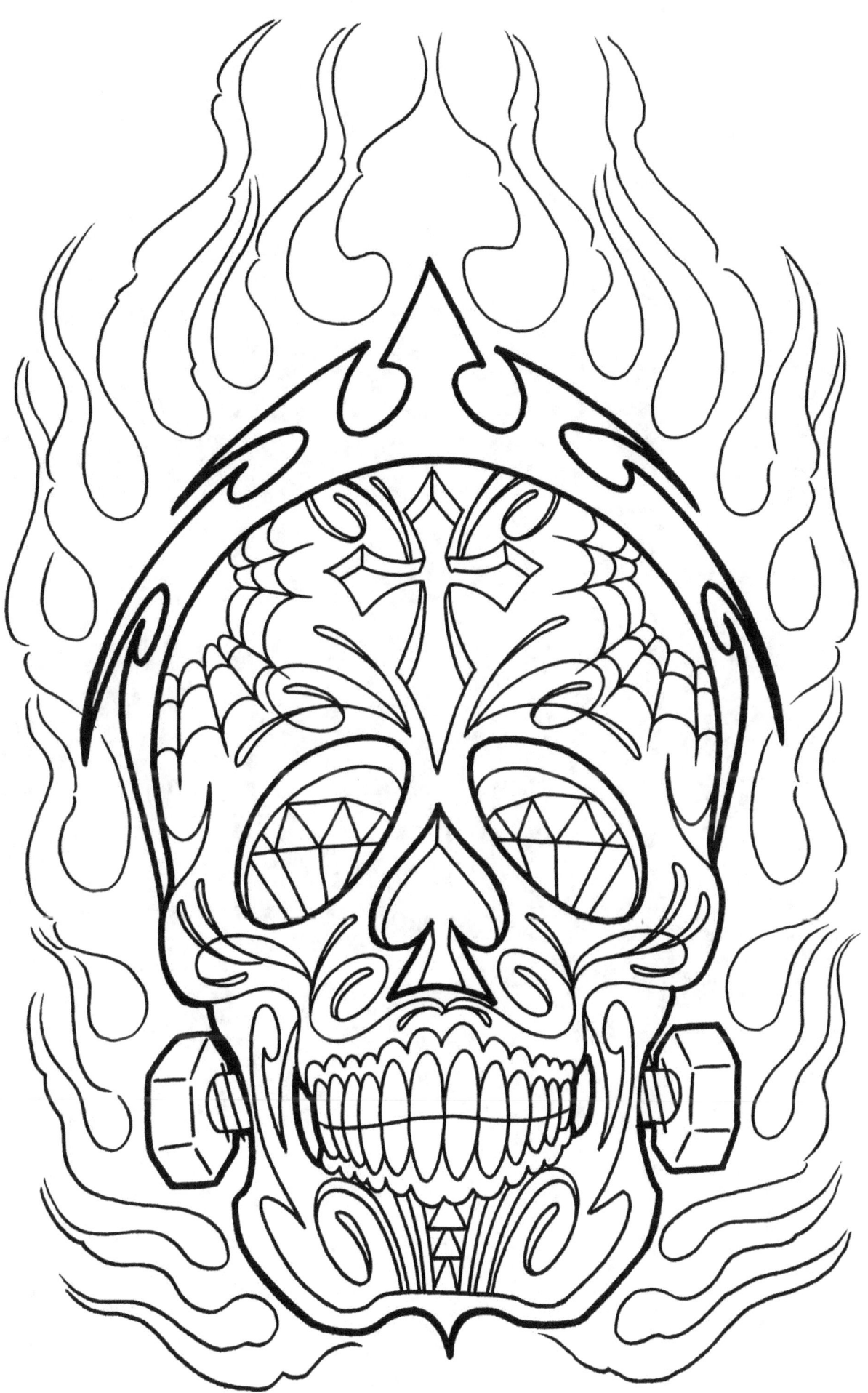

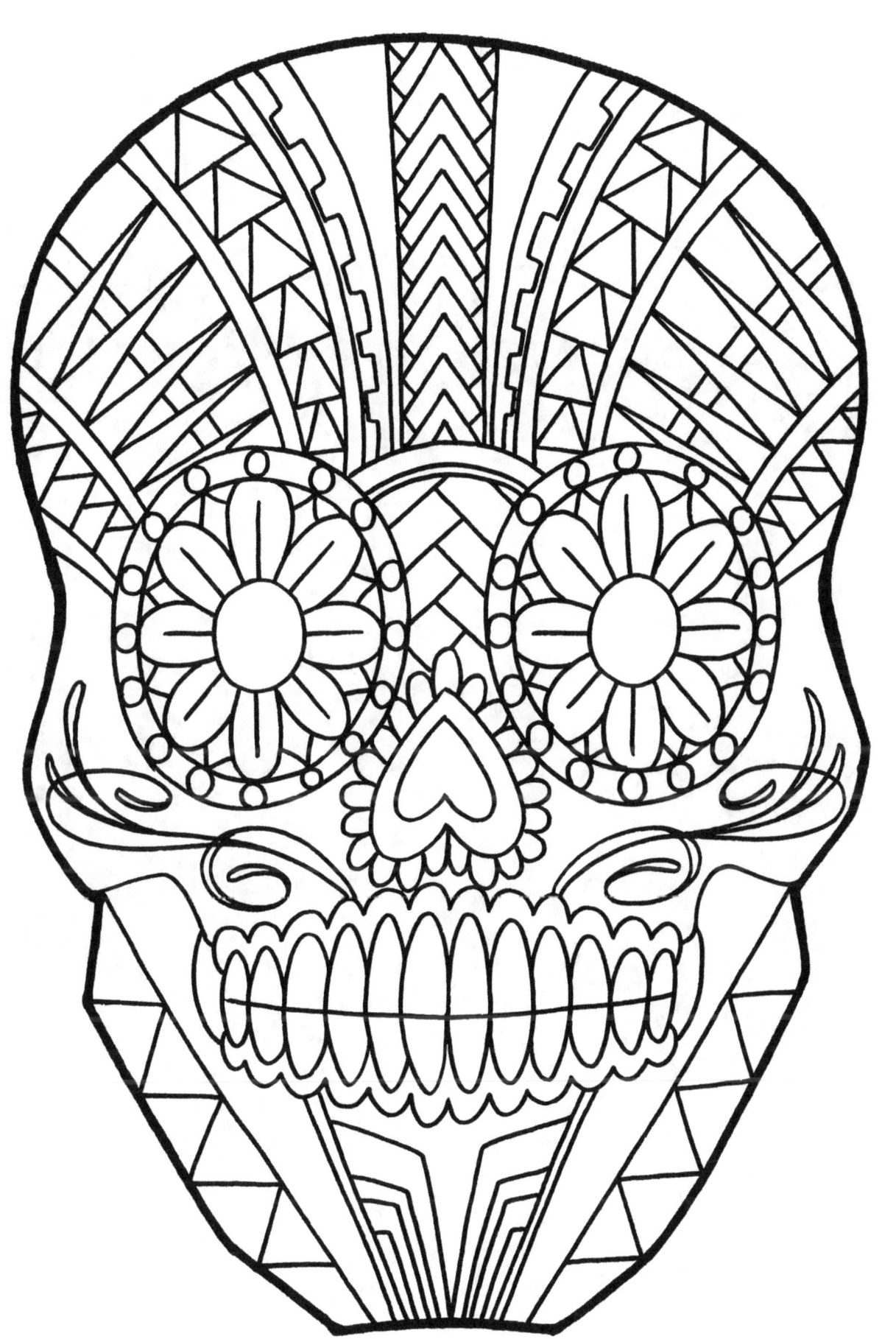

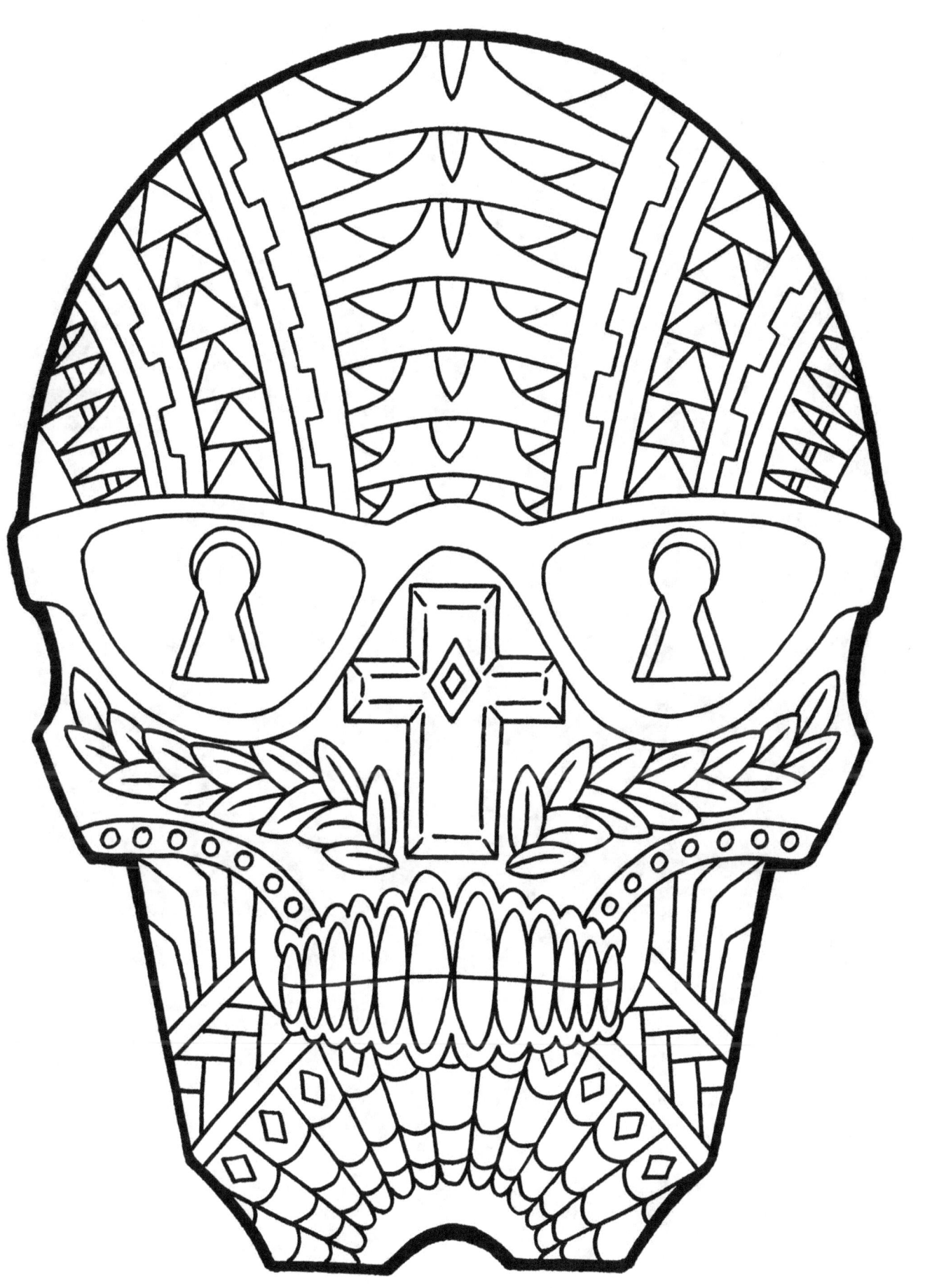

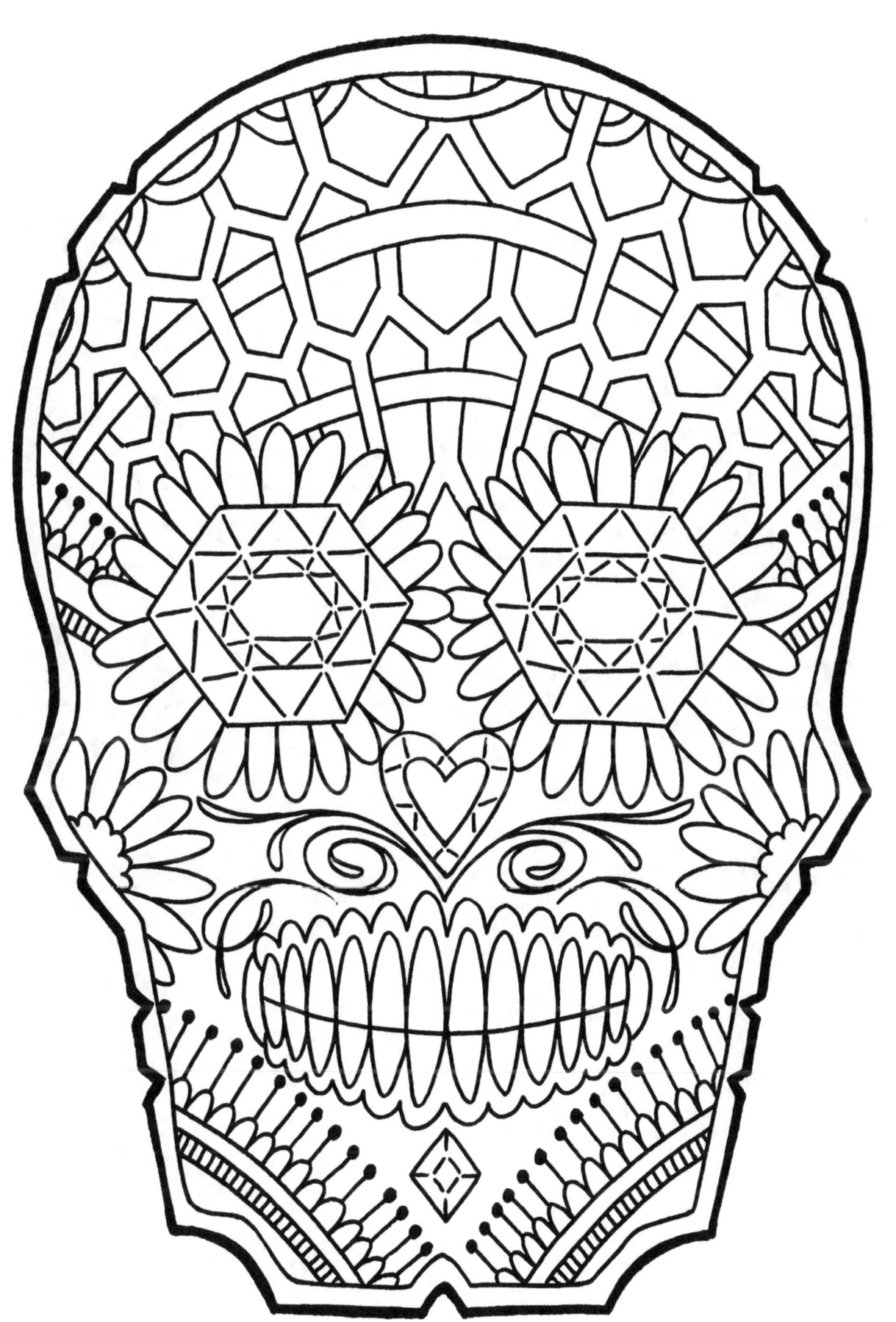

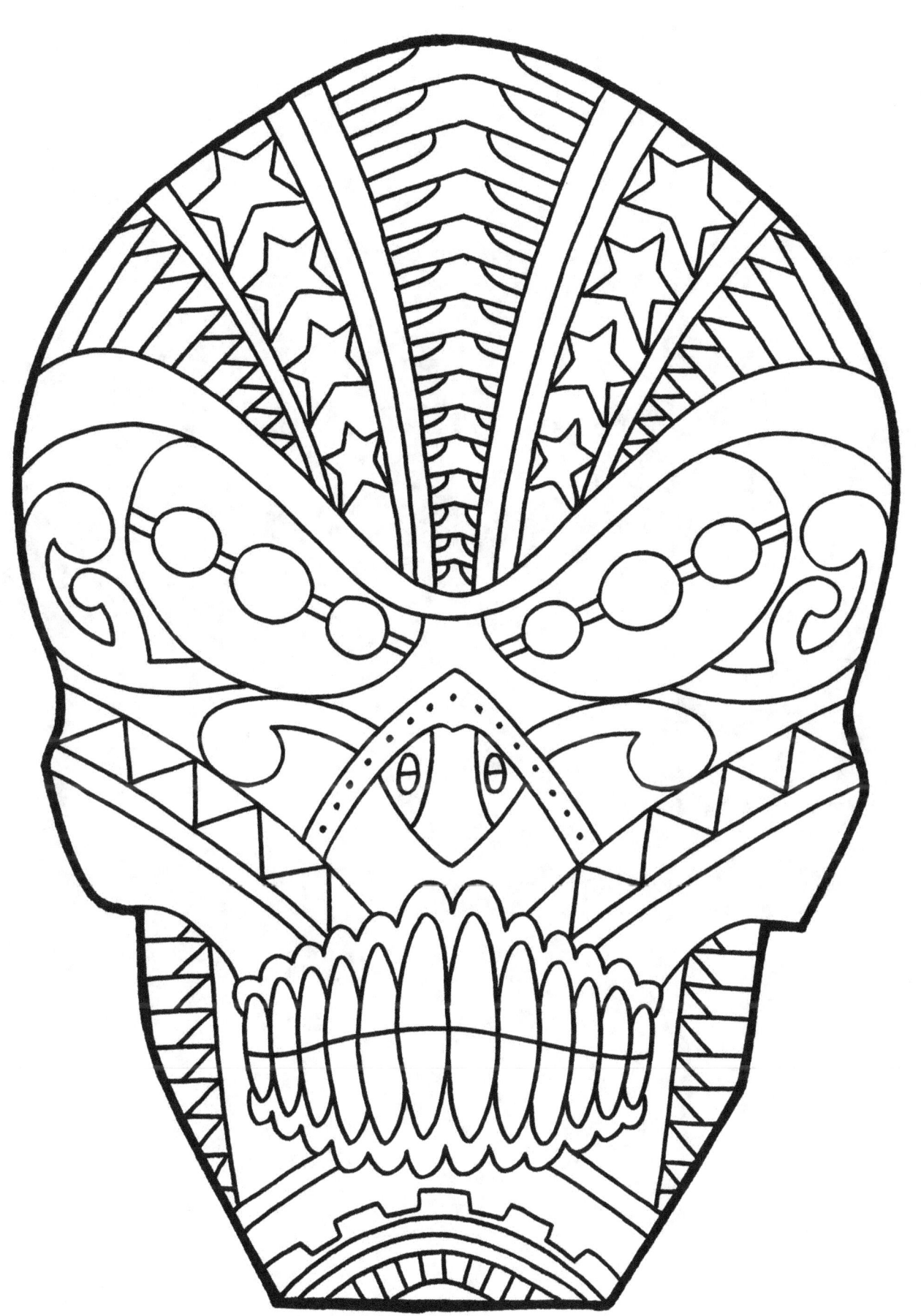

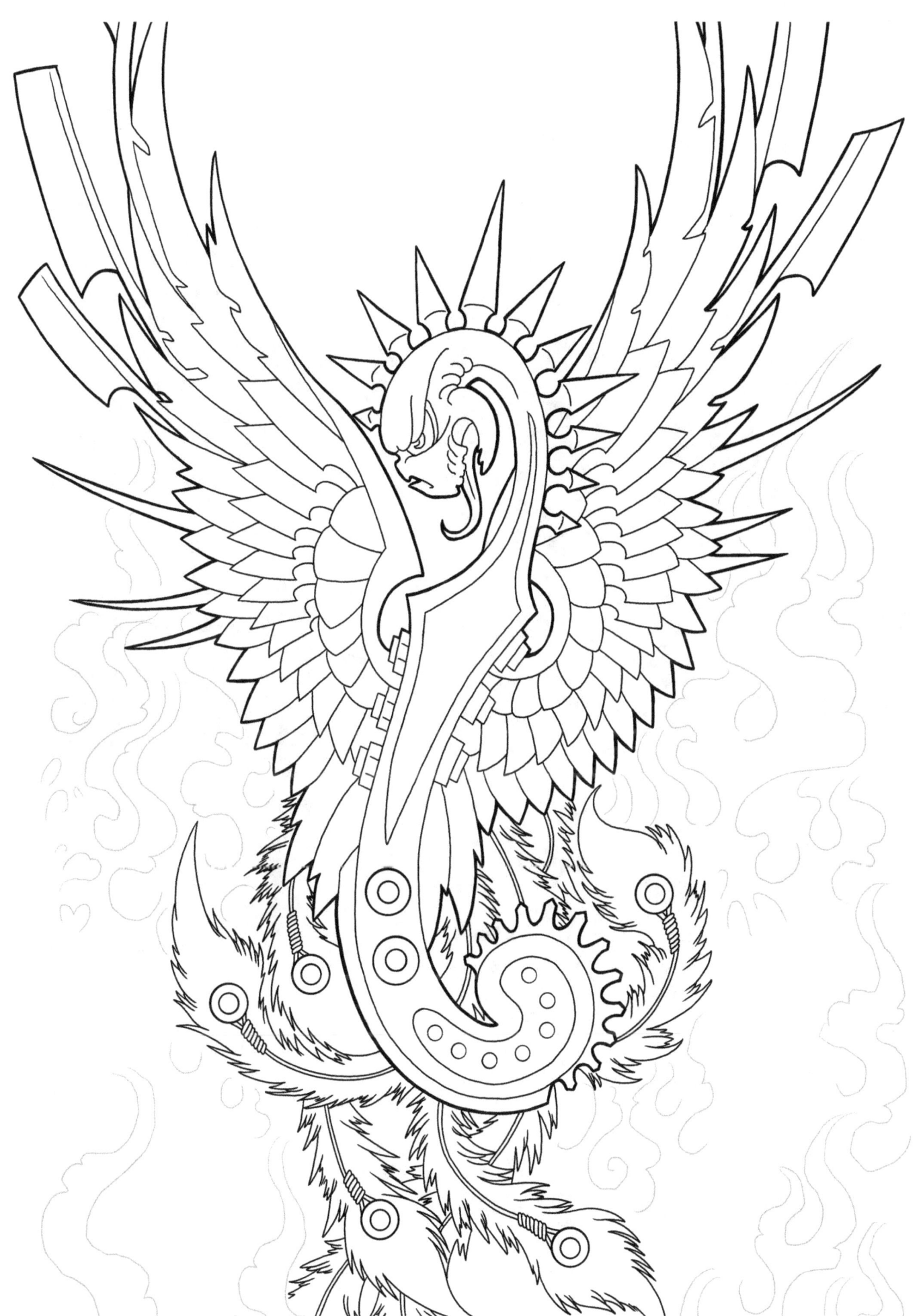

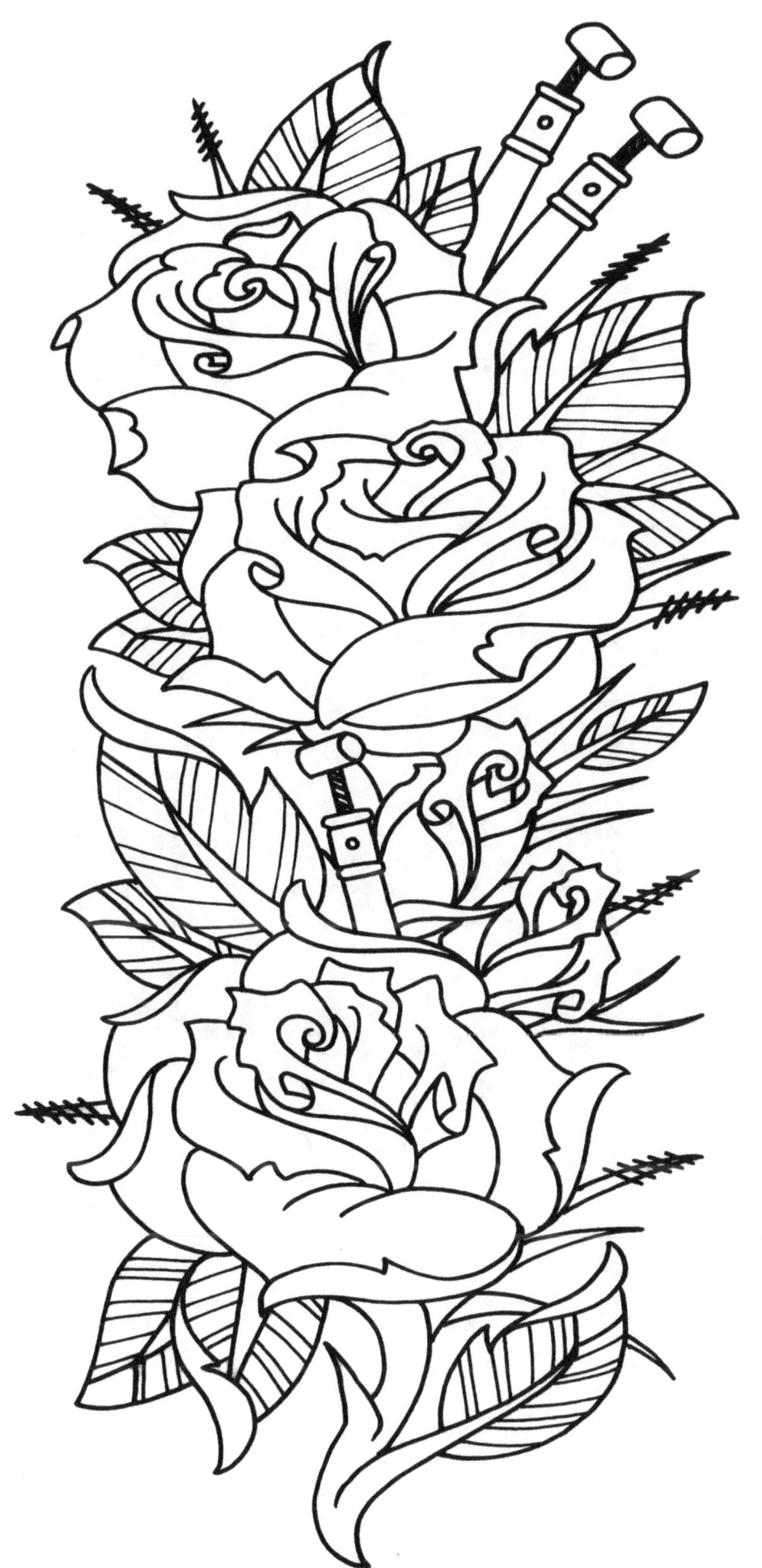

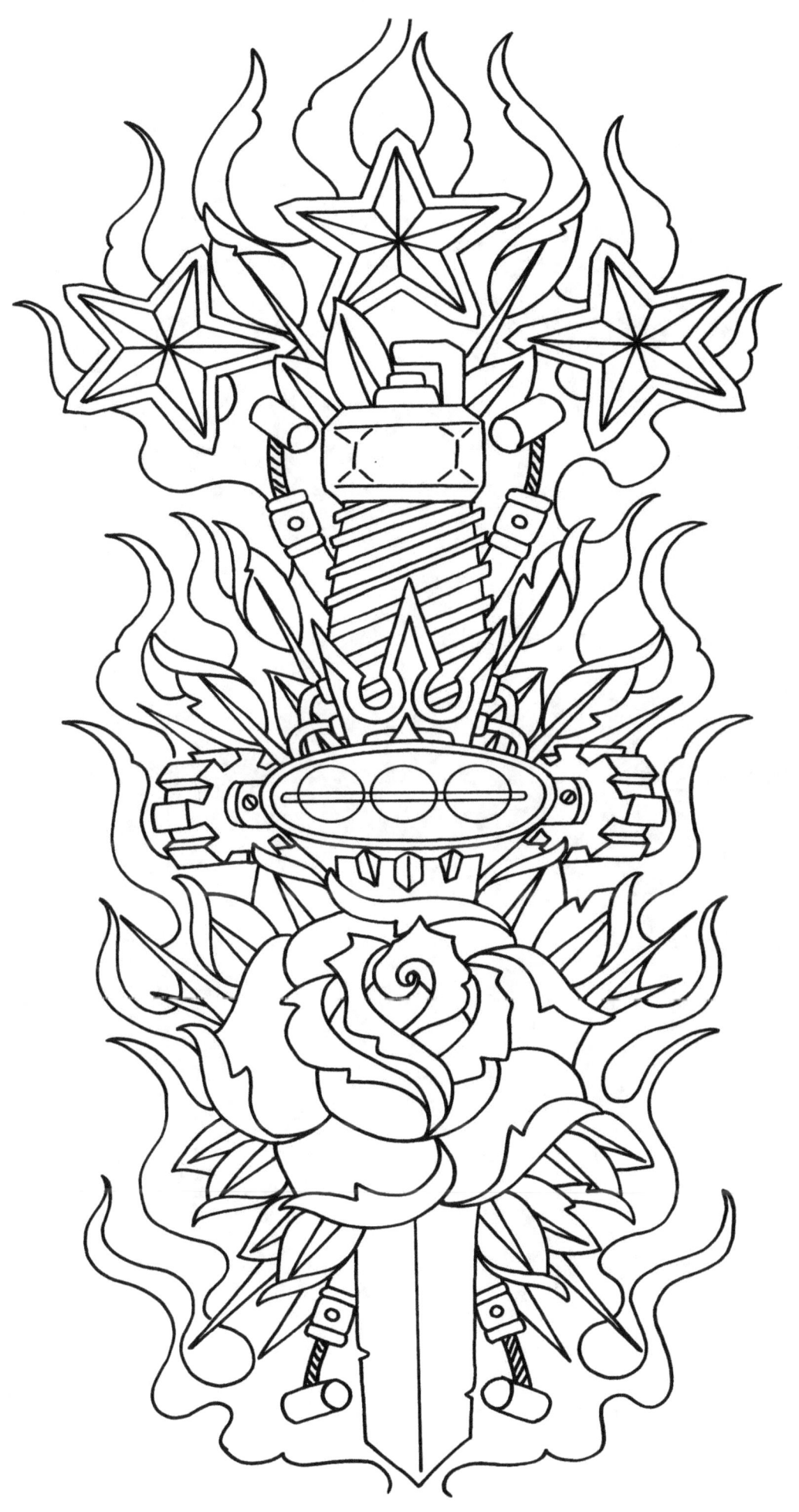

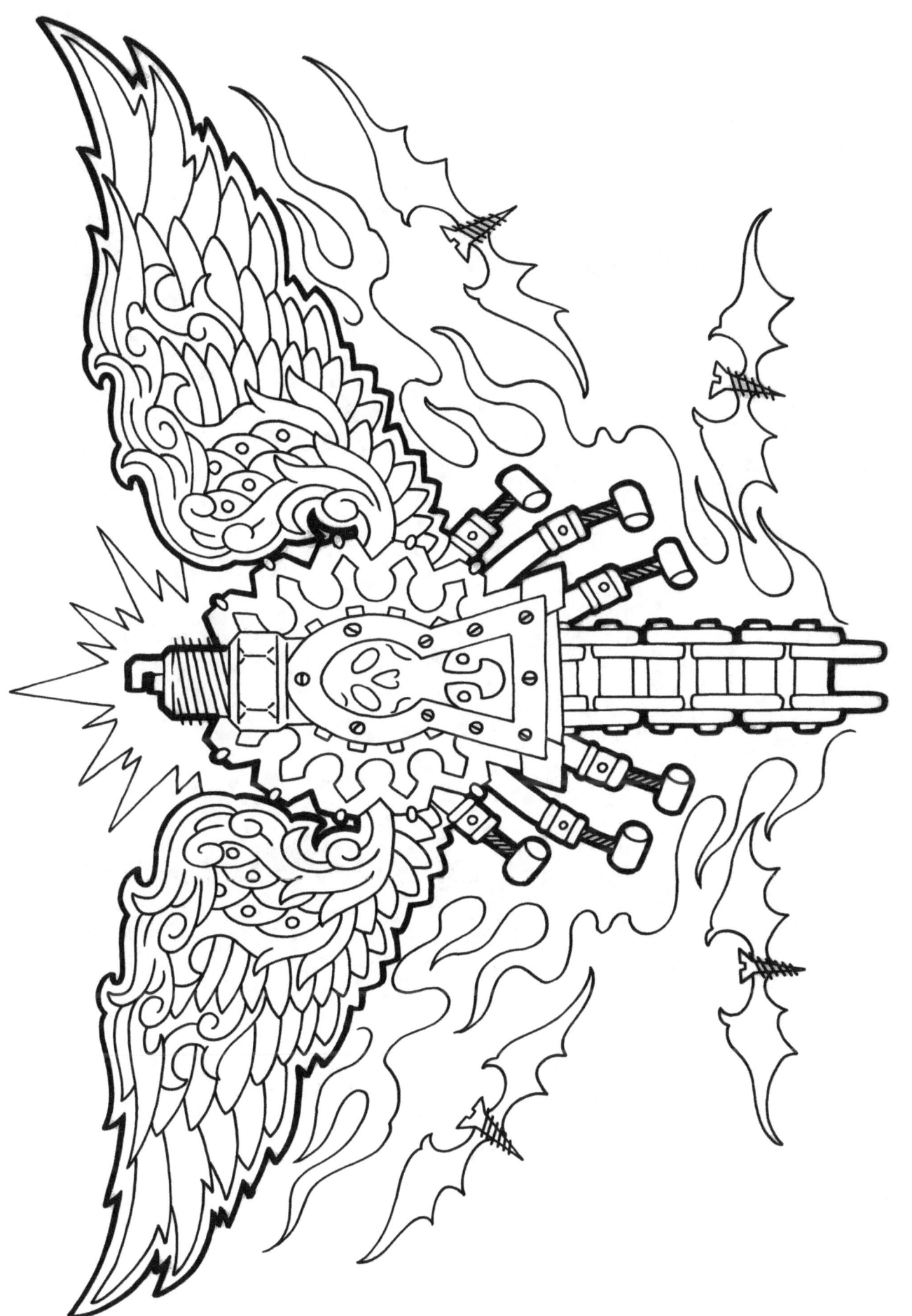

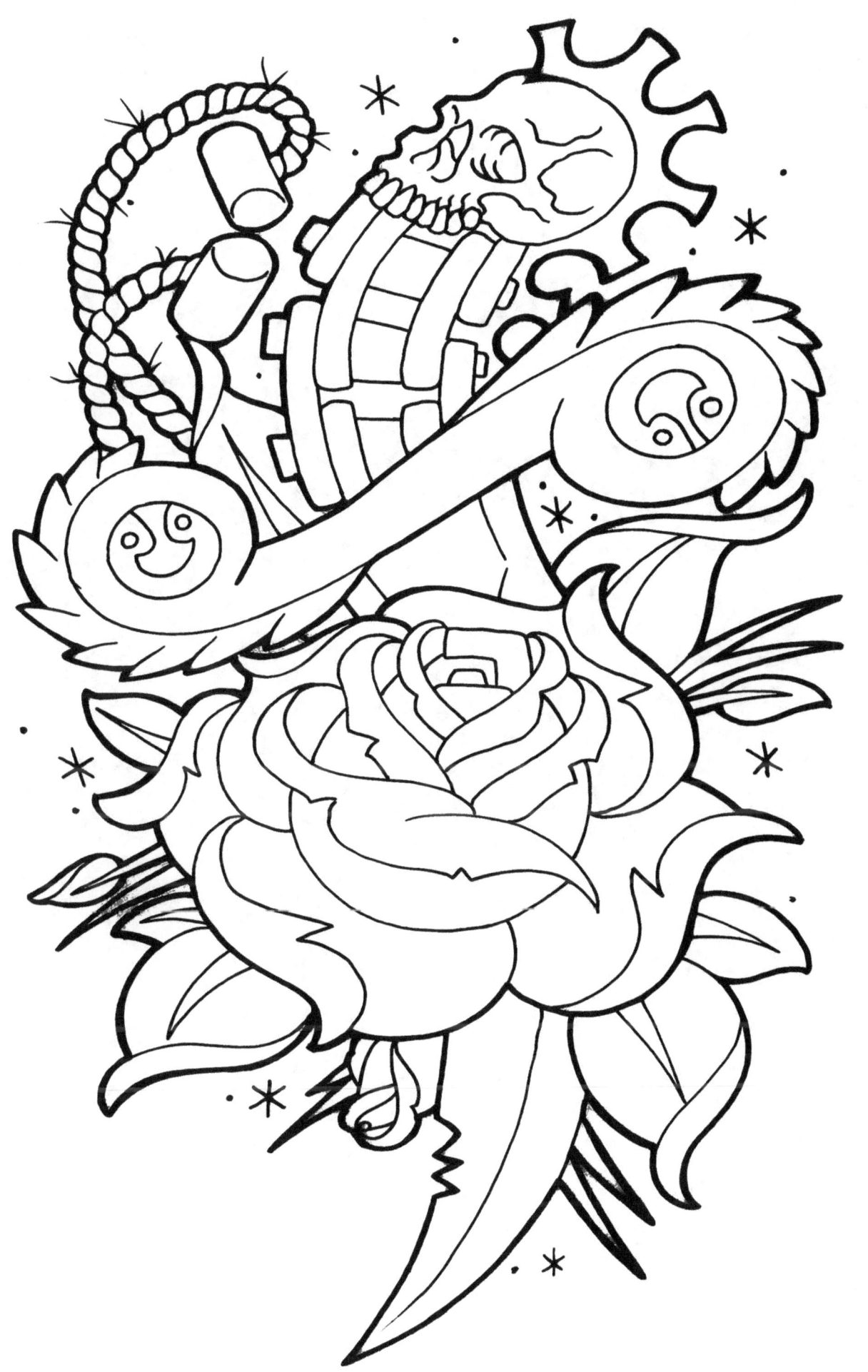

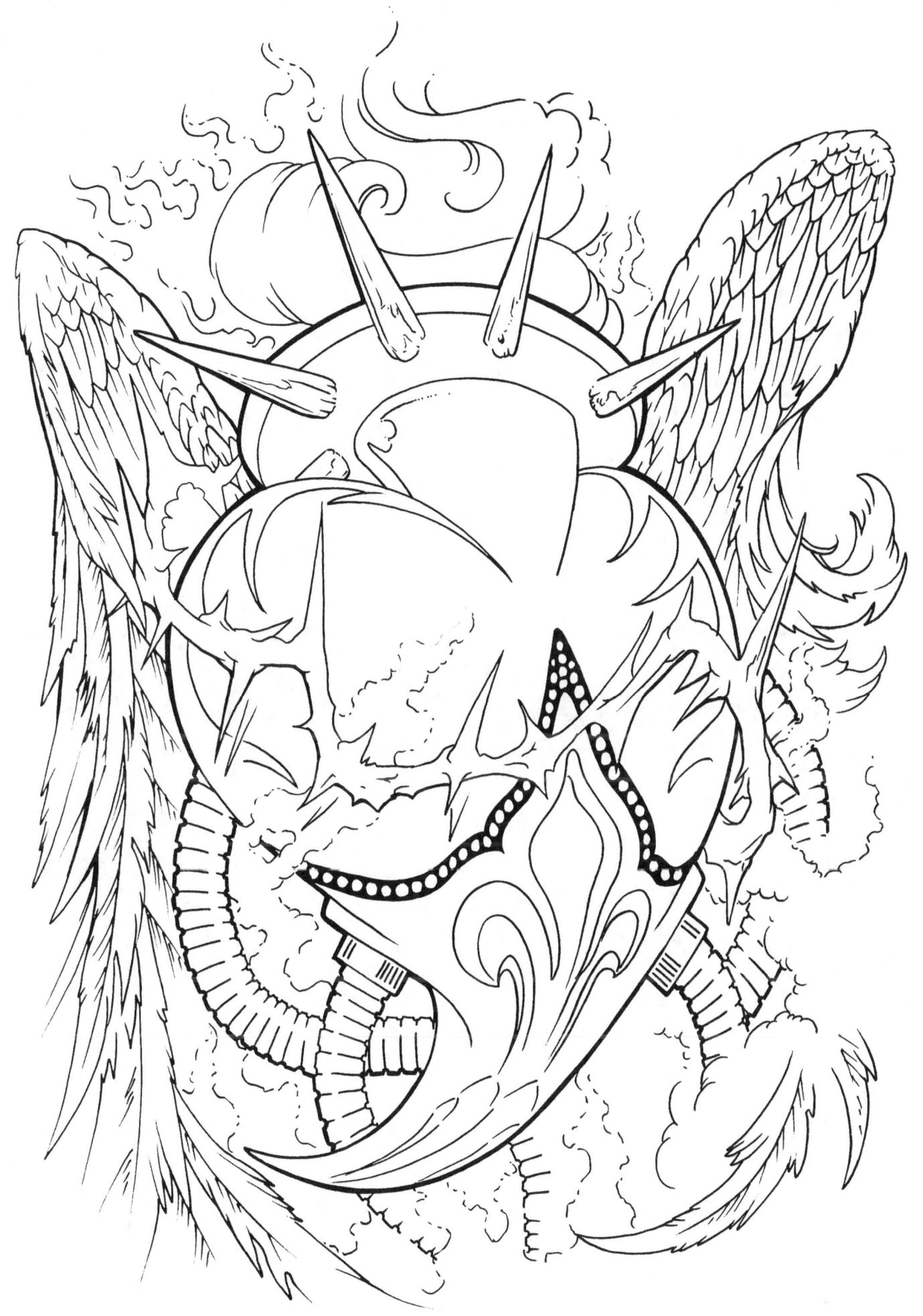

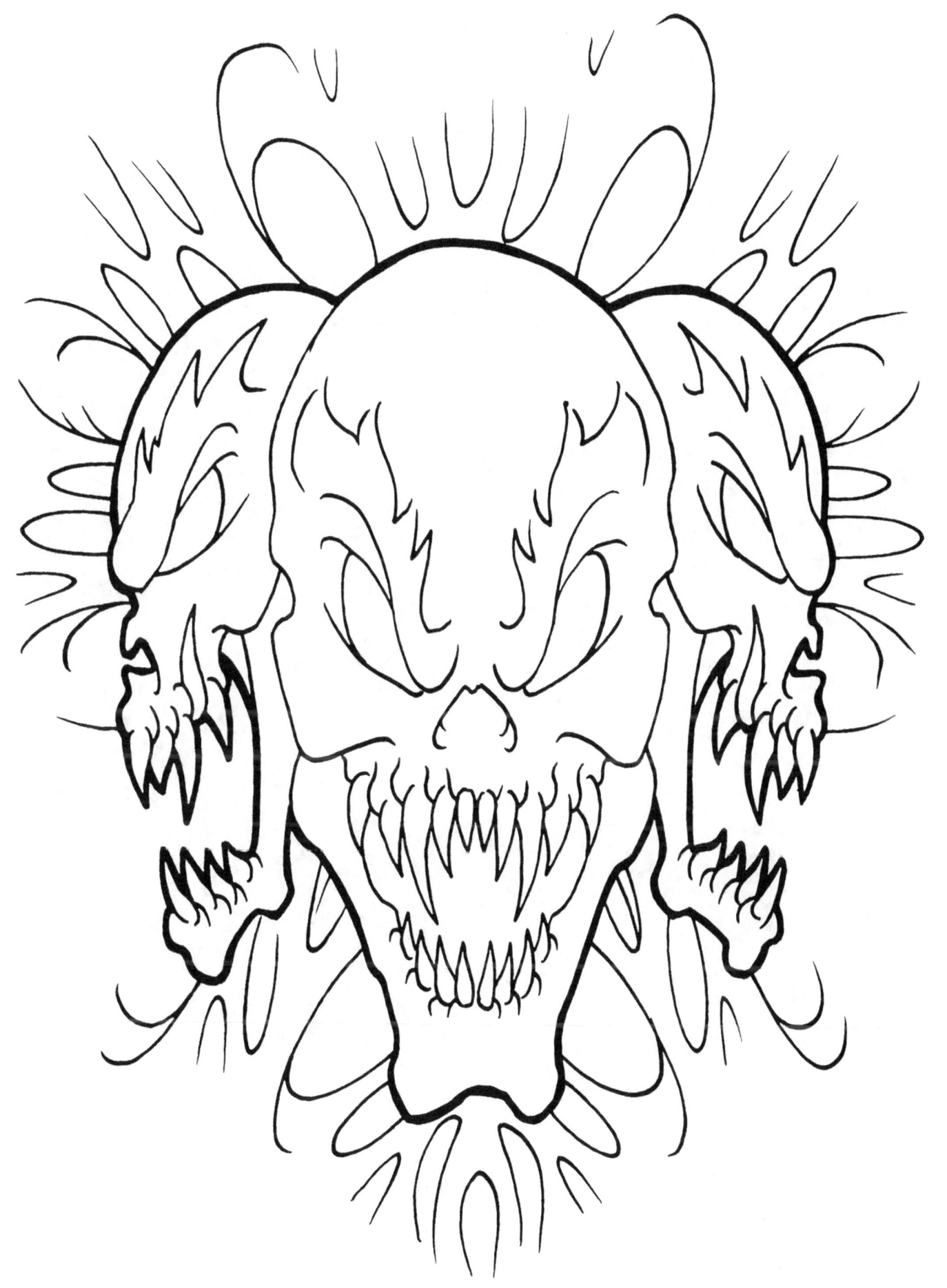

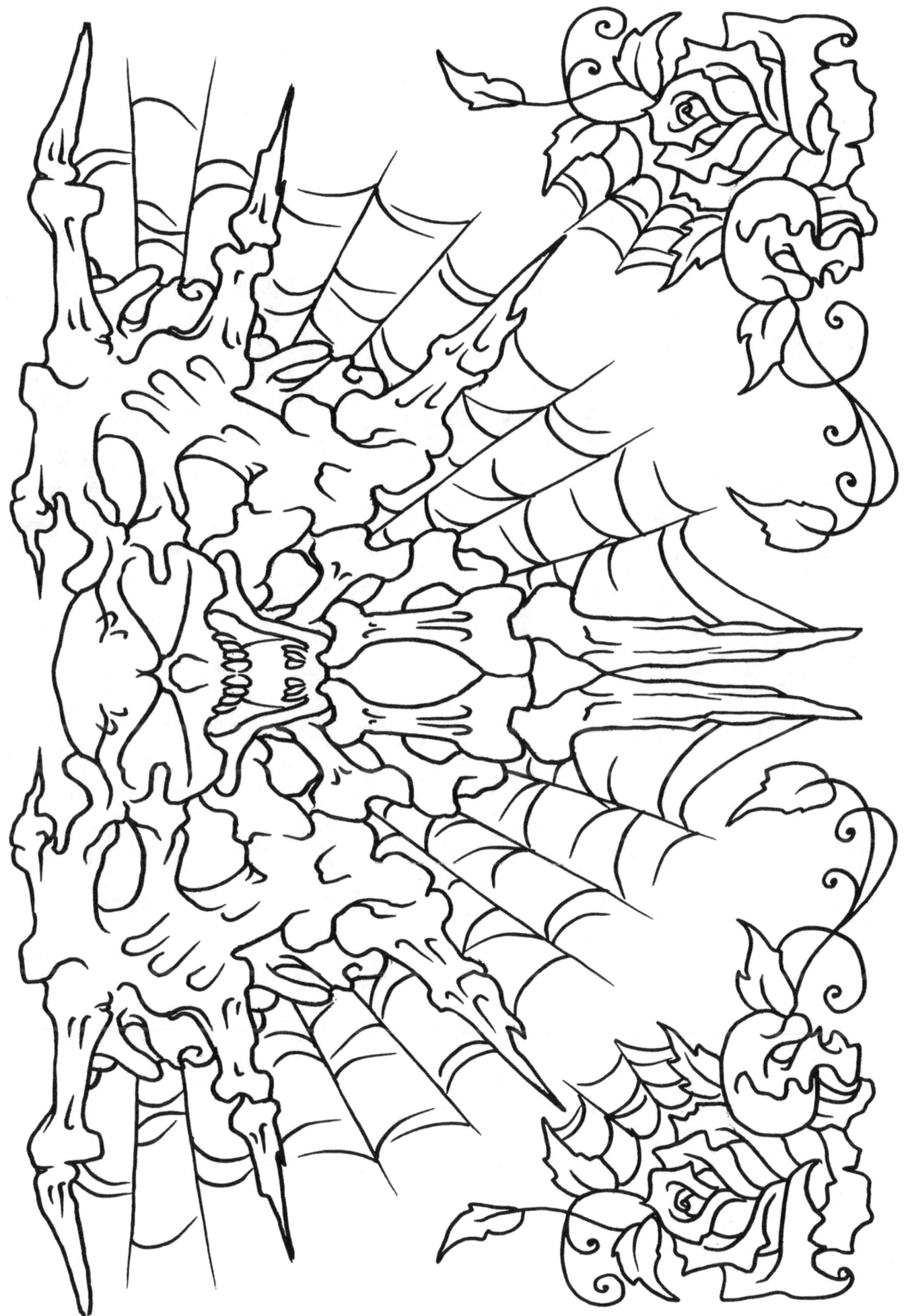

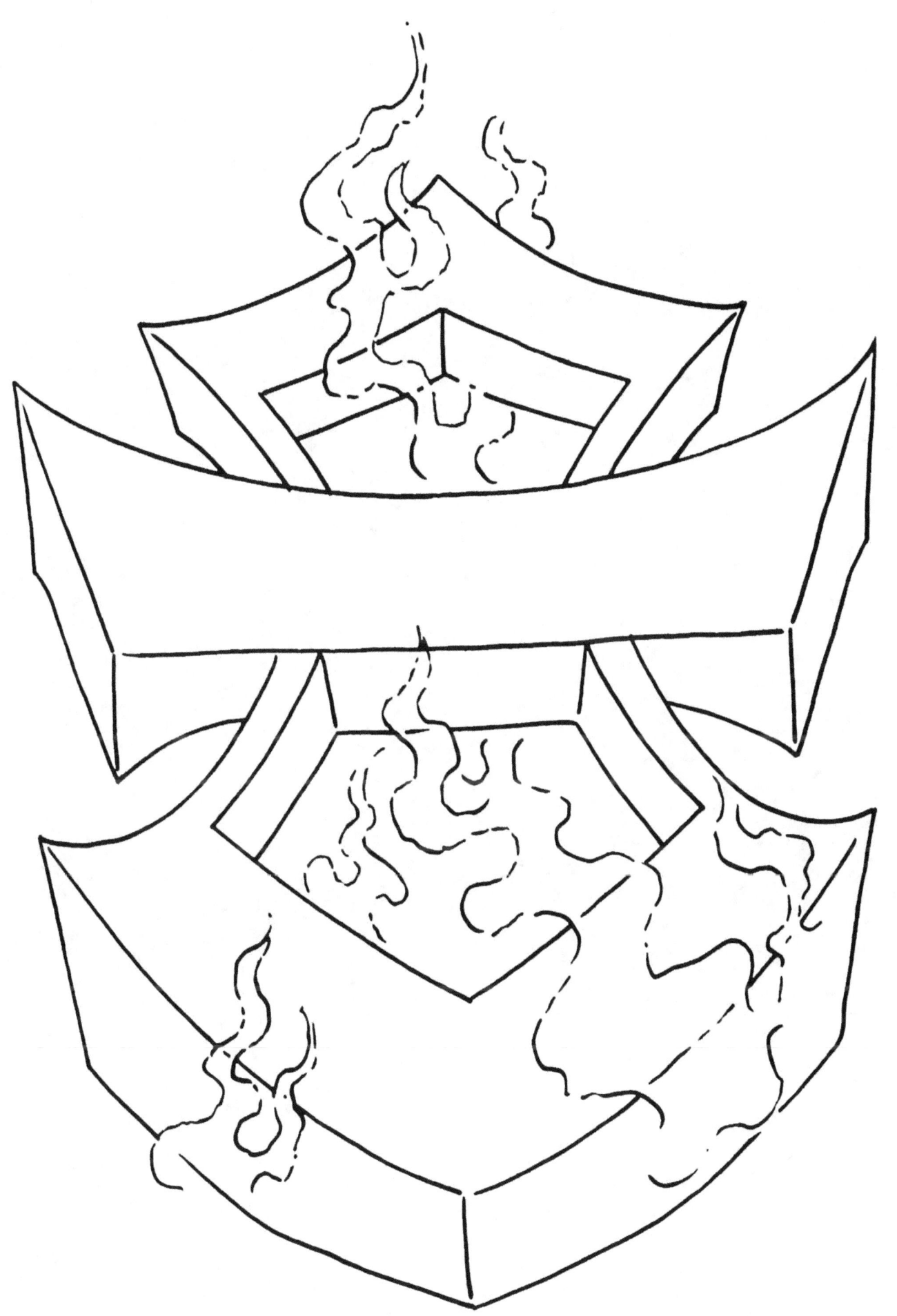

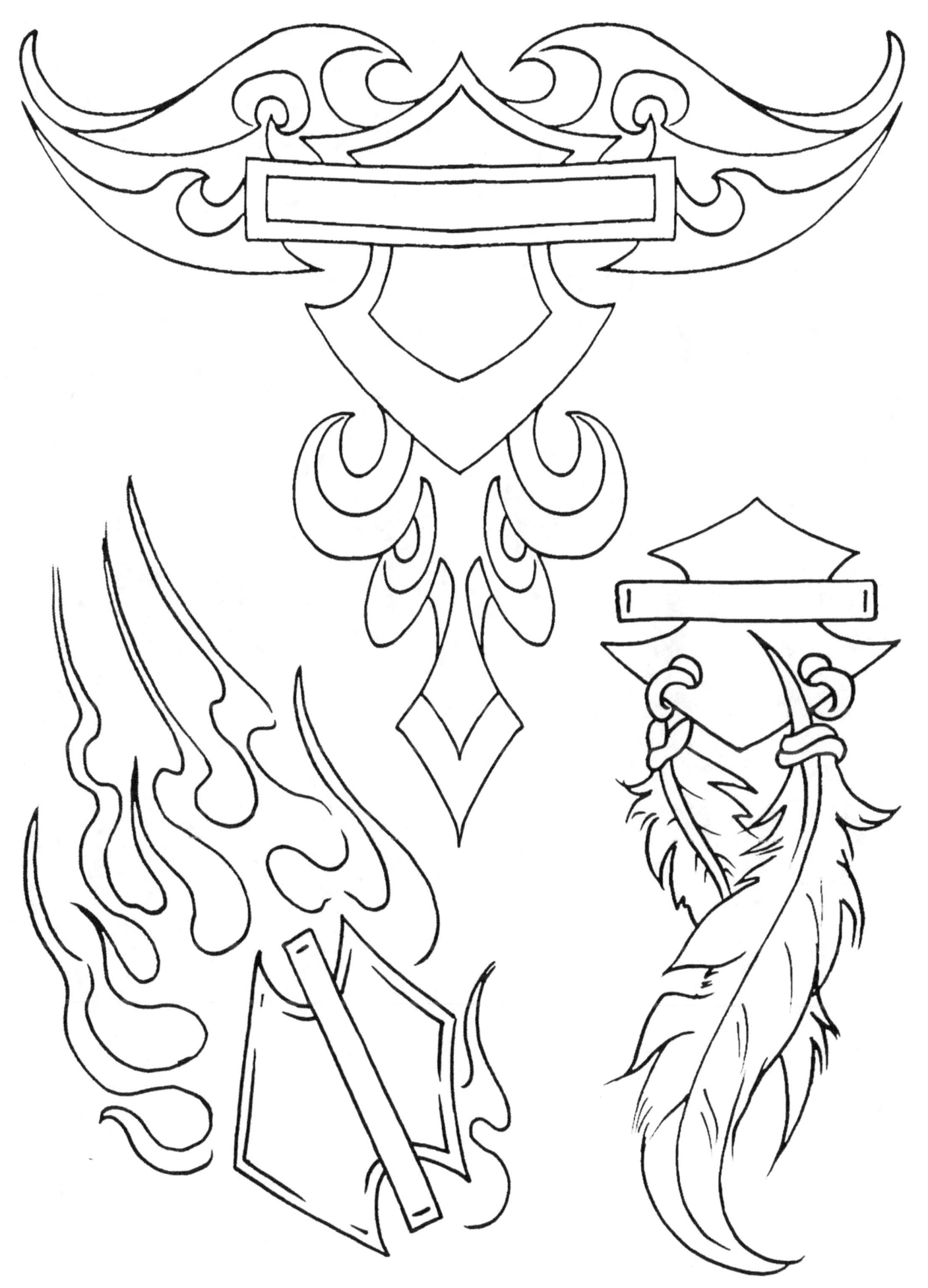

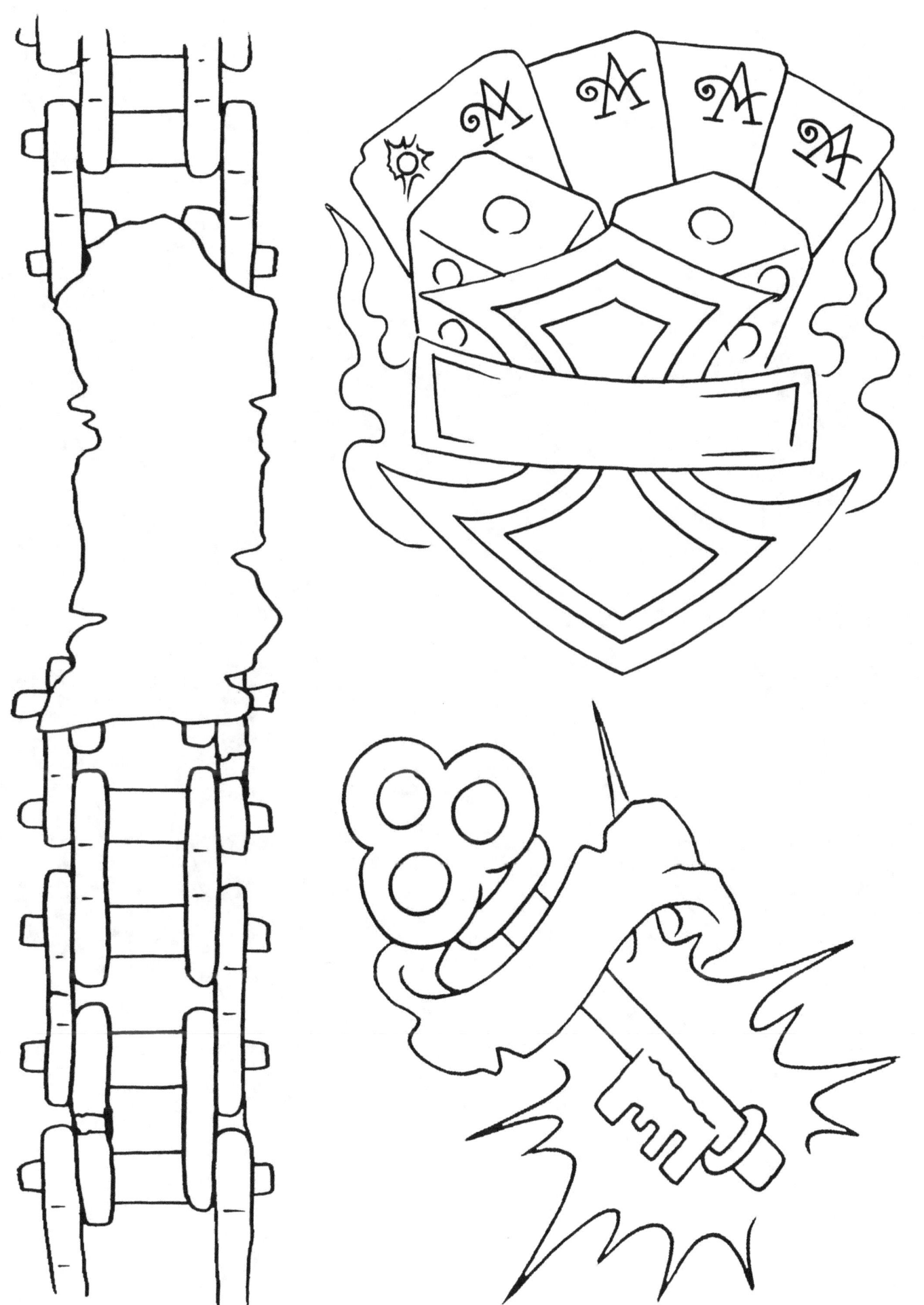

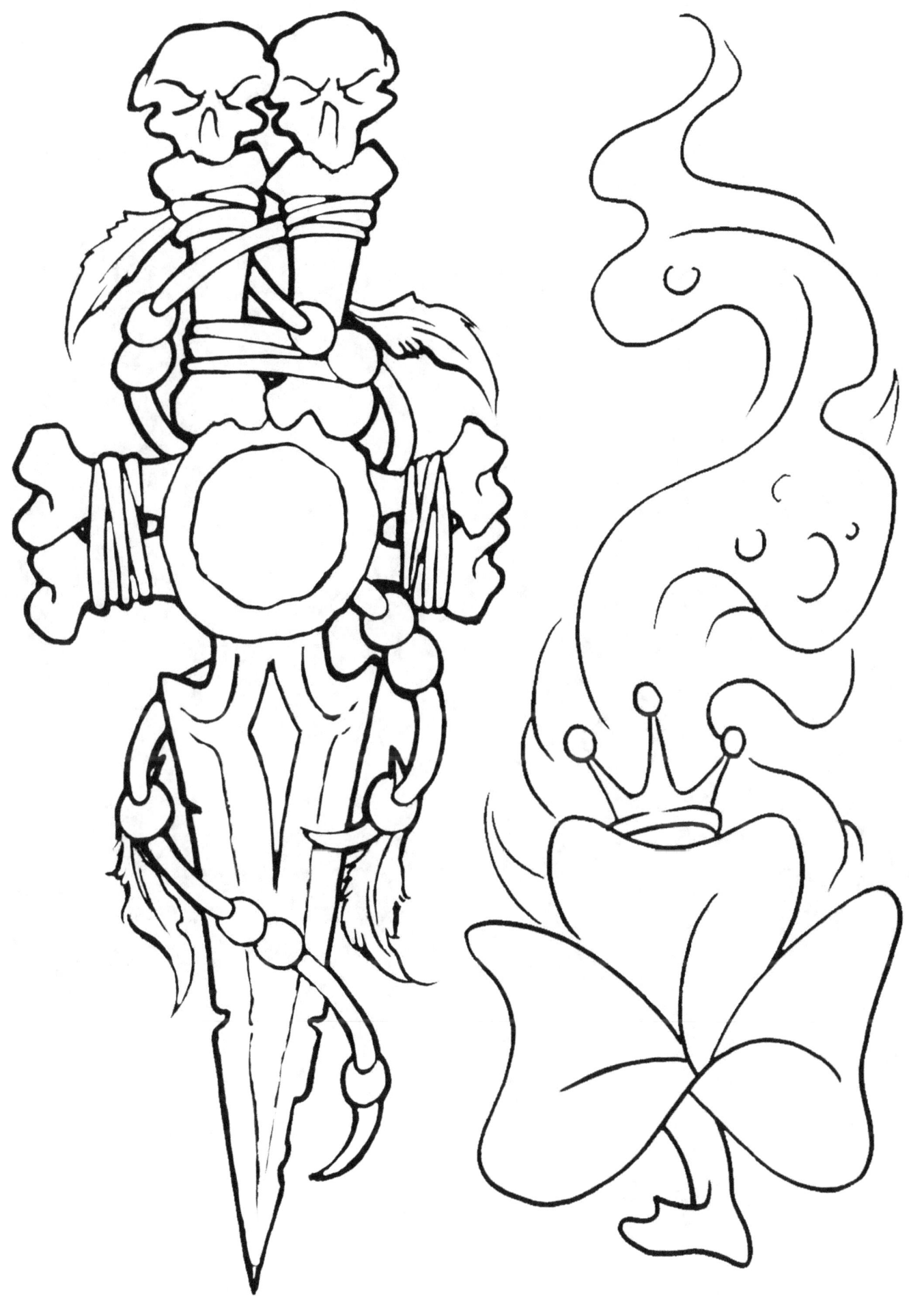

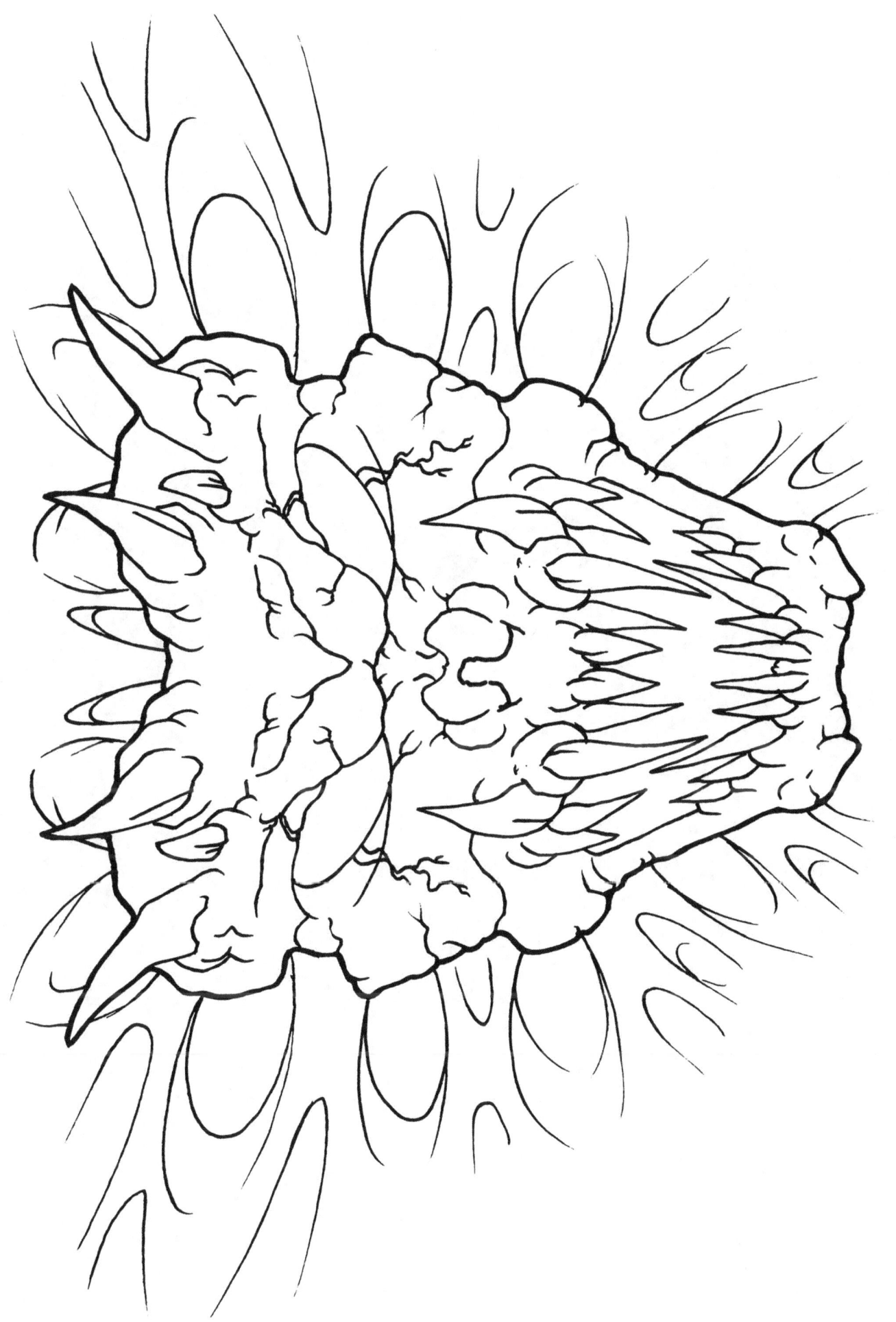

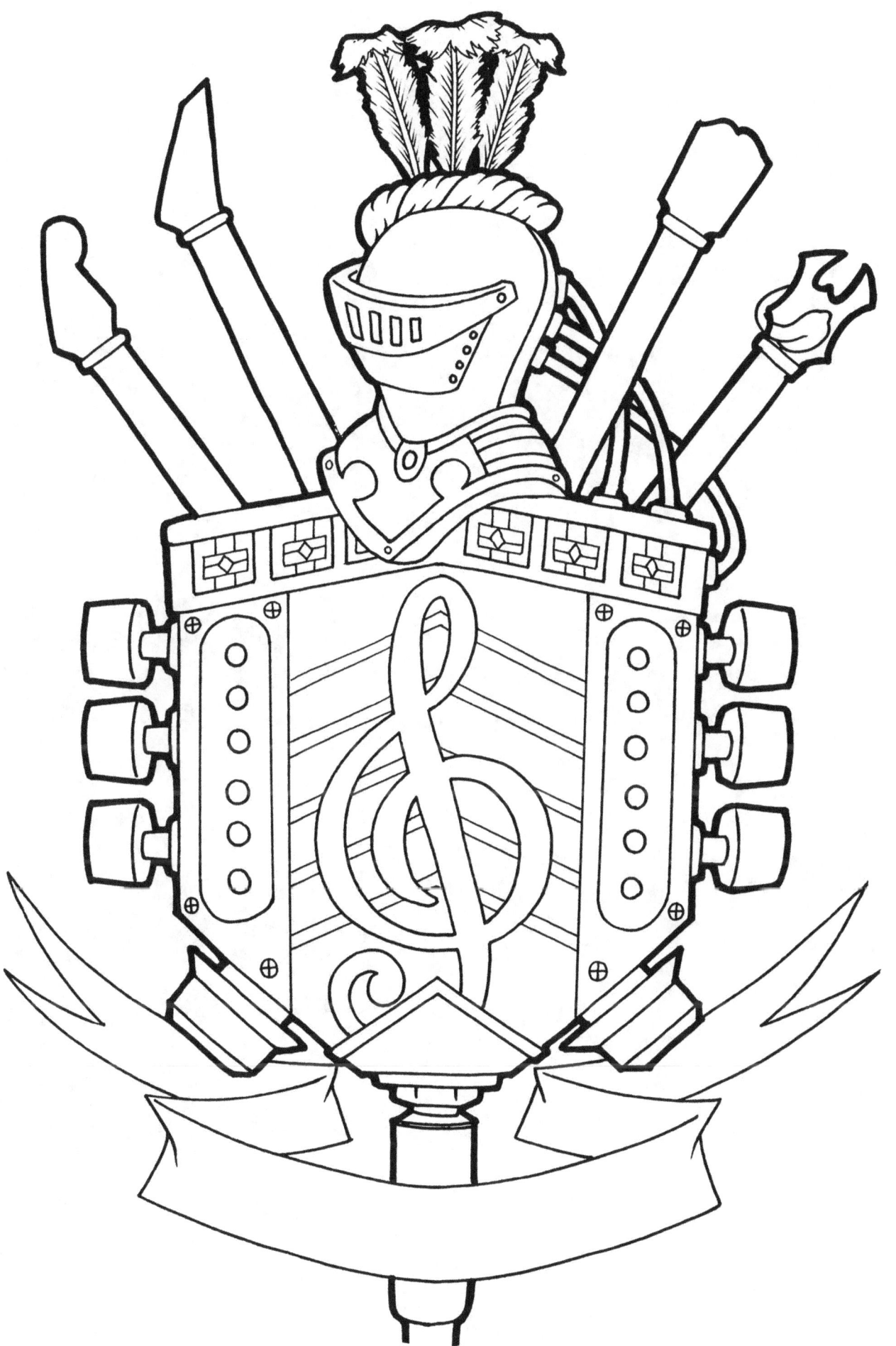

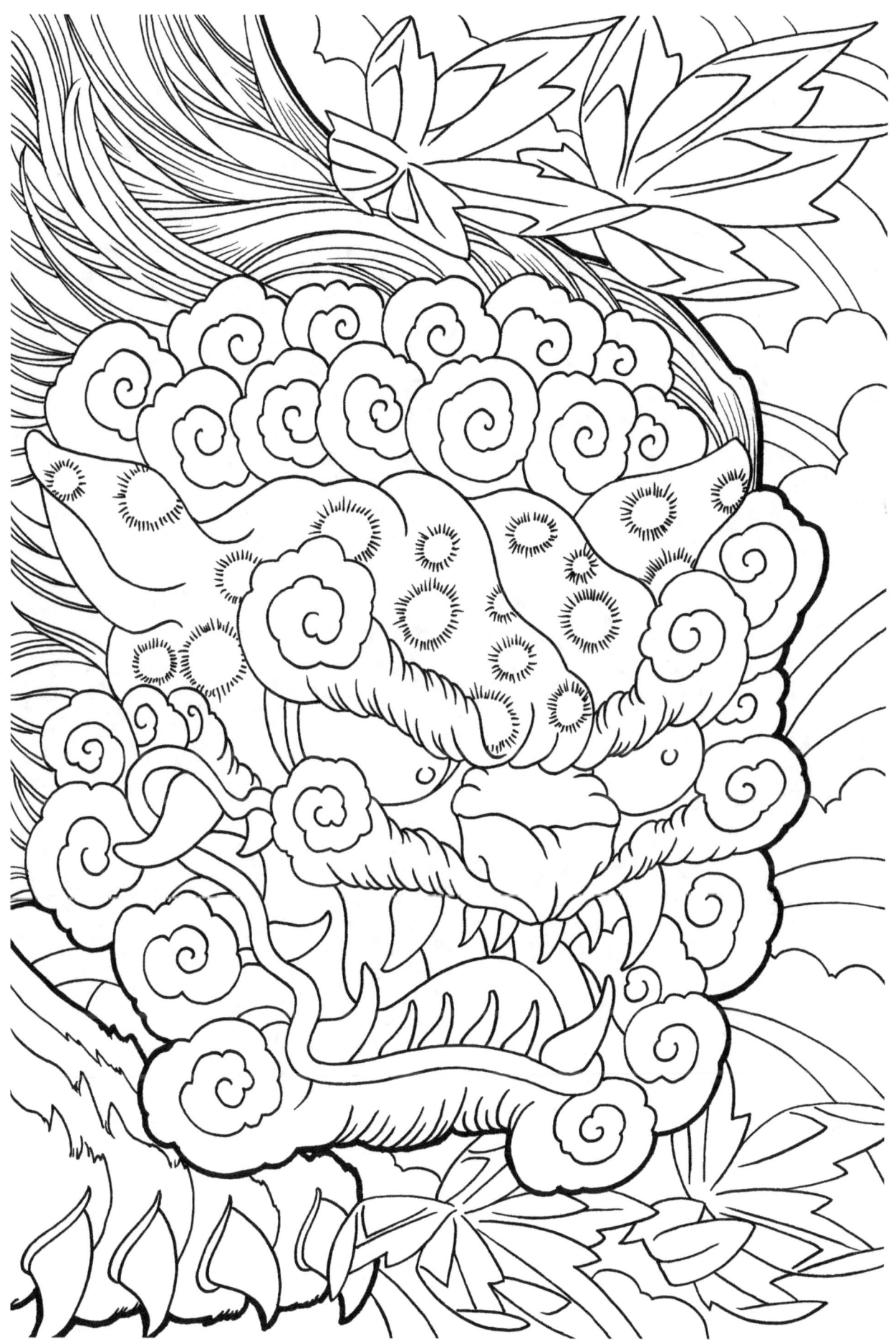

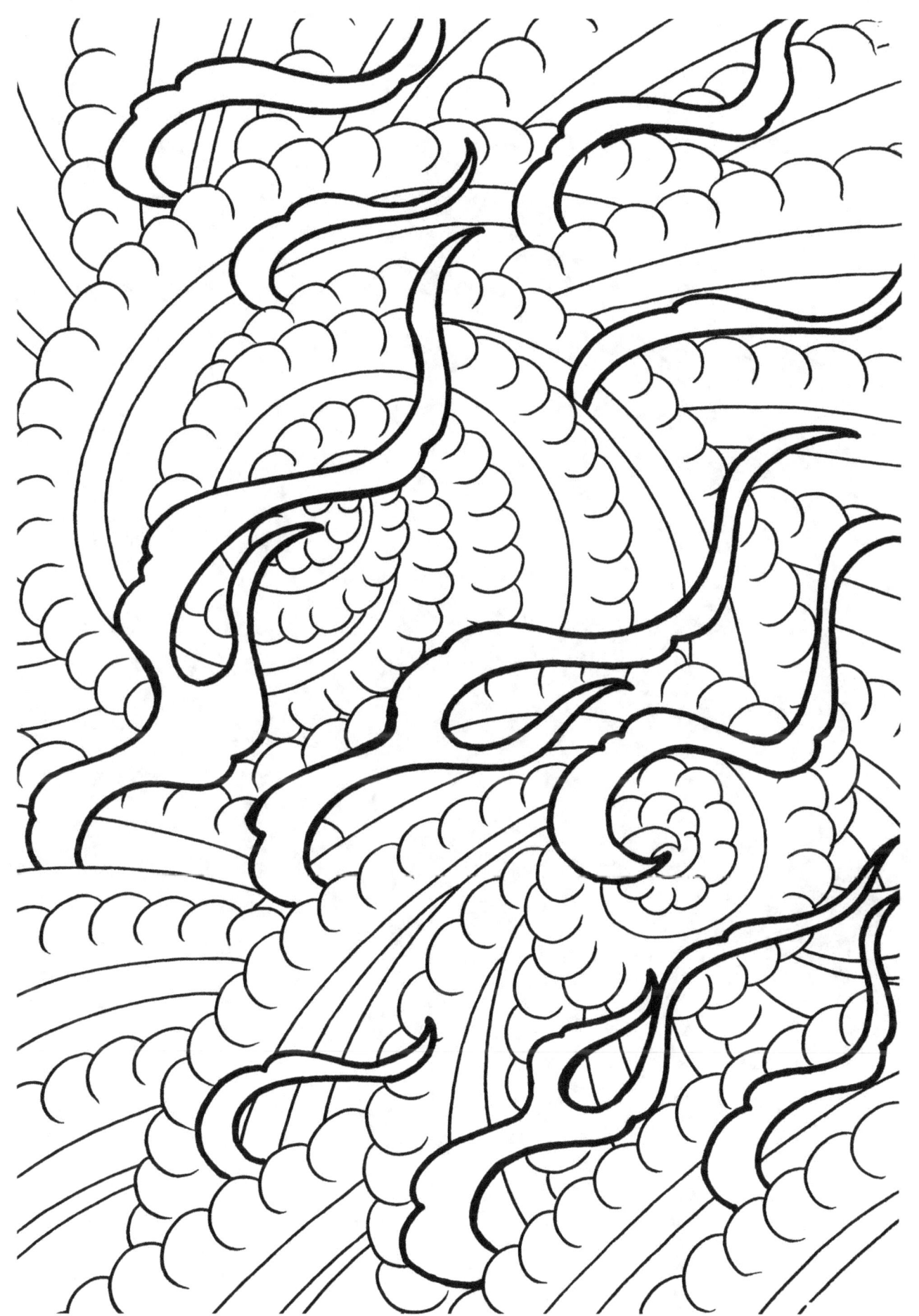

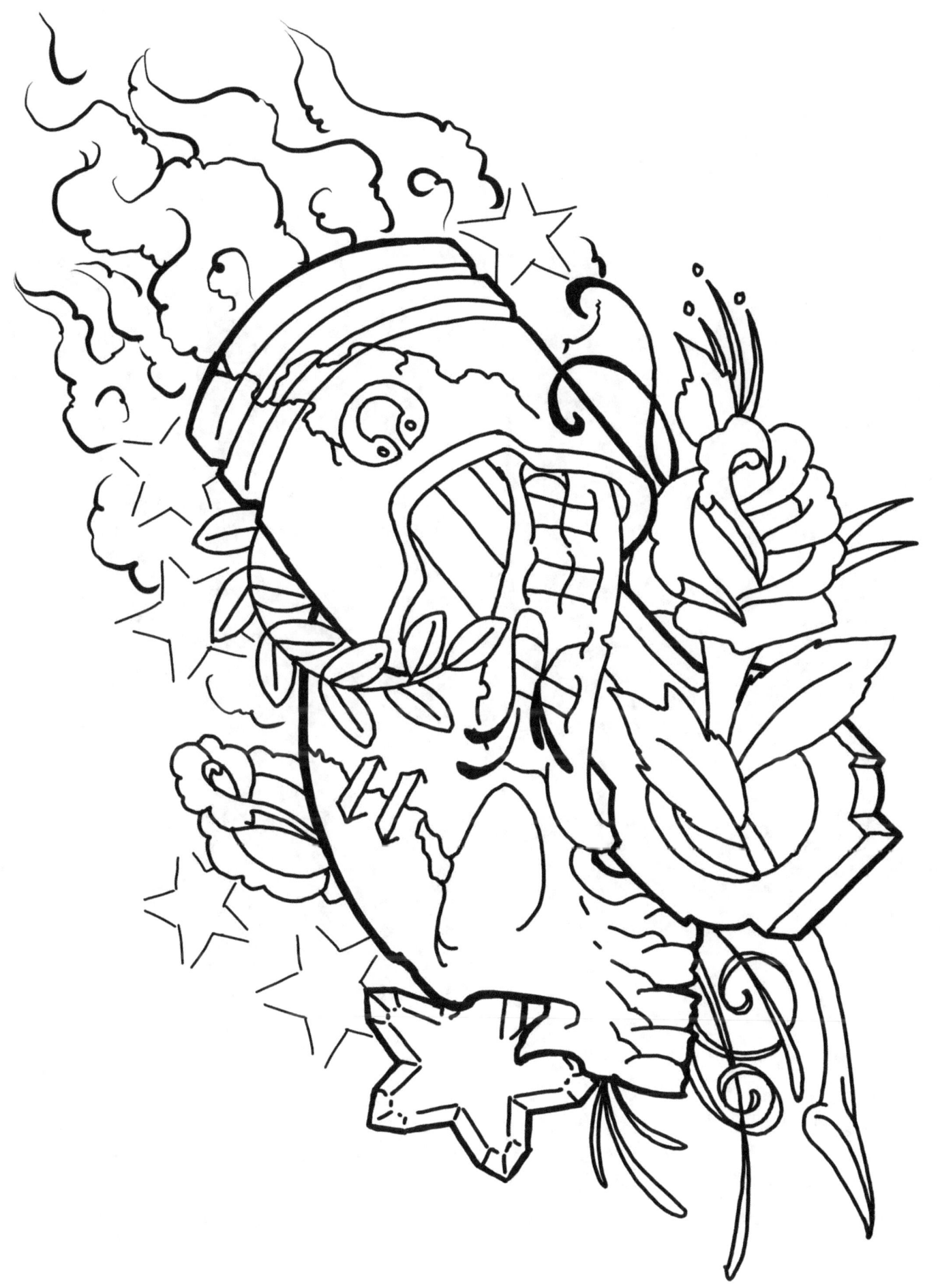

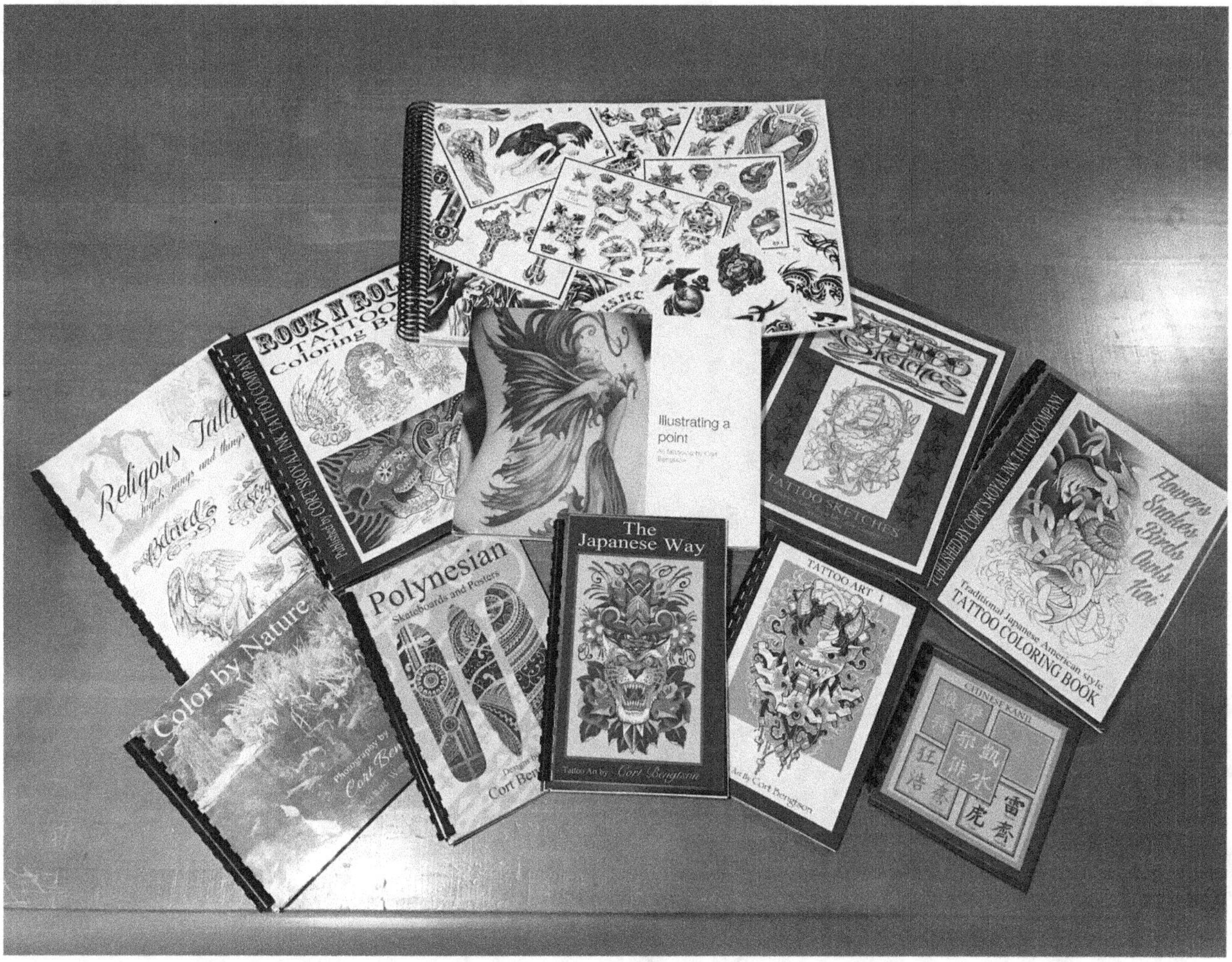

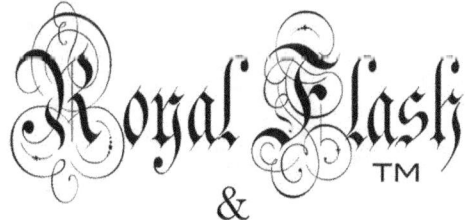

From Japanese style to surreal black and gray,
to watercolors and computer art, we have
something you will love. Prints
ranging in size from 11" x 17" to
40" x 50" will adjust the visual appeal
of any room.

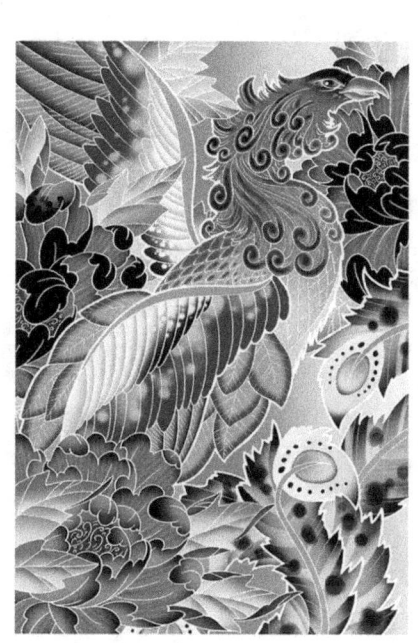
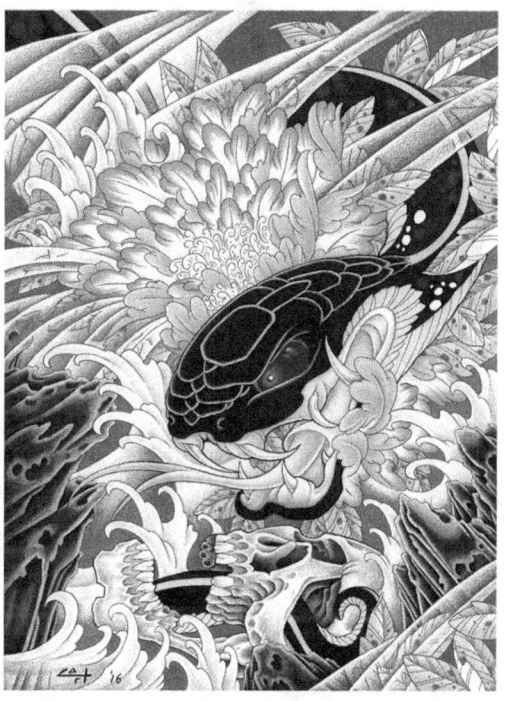
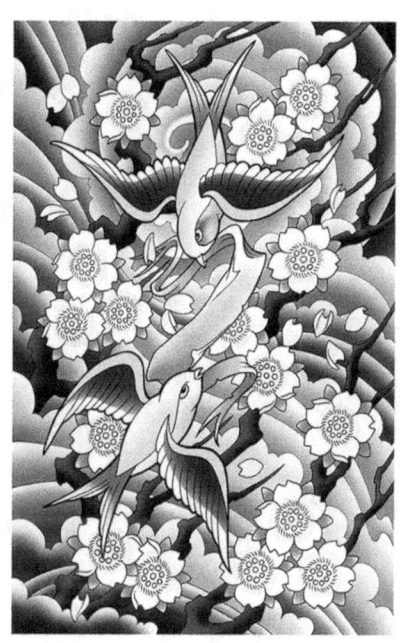
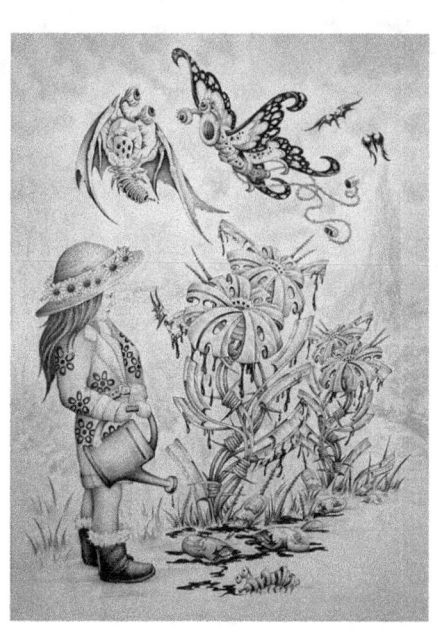
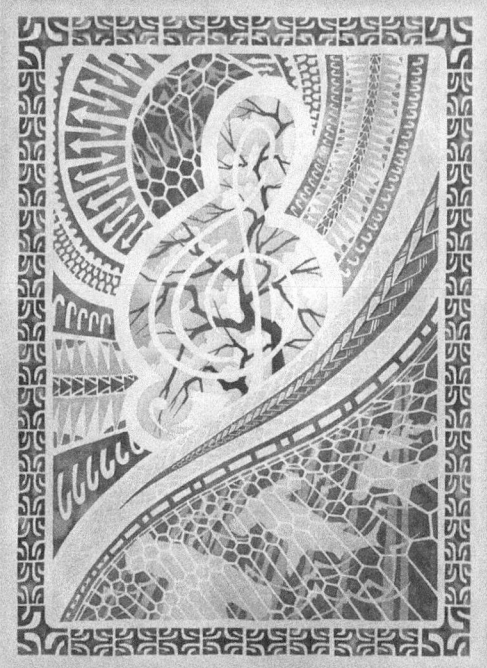
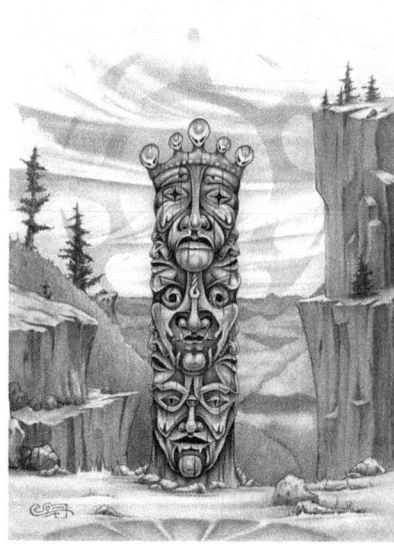

www.ingramcontent.com/pod-product-compliance
Lightning Source LLC
Chambersburg PA
CBHW081740220526
45468CB00008B/2177